Getting
Closer *to* God

Getting Closer to God

Lessons from the Life of Moses

ERWIN W. LUTZER

Kregel
Publications

Getting Closer to God: Lessons from the Life of Moses
© 2000, 2011 by Erwin Lutzer

Published by Kregel Publications, a division of Kregel, Inc.,
P.O. Box 2607, Grand Rapids, MI 49501.

ISBN 978-0-8254-4195-0

Printed in the United States of America

14 15 / 5 4 3 2

To
Bruce Richard,
our first son-in-law,
whose devotion to God
and love for our daughter Lorisa
makes our hearts glad.

Contents

Preface

Though God is everywhere, we are still invited to "draw near" to develop our confidence in Him, enjoy His company, and experience His presence. In the Bible, God is often pictured as One who is nearer to some people than others; sometimes He extends His hand, at other times He hides His face. We've probably experienced both responses.

When the psalmist wanted to tell us about the relationship Moses had with God, he wrote, "He made known His ways to Moses, His acts to the sons of Israel" (Ps 103:7). While the vast multitude of Israelites saw only God's outward deeds, Moses saw God's character, beauty, and faithfulness.

No person on earth has ever enjoyed the intimacy Moses had with God. "Thus the Lord used to speak to Moses face to face, just as a man speaks to his friend" (Ex 33:11). No one spent more time with God; no one understood Him better.

Moses was born in a dark period of Hebrew history. A cruel Pharaoh arose who forced the Israelites to be slaves, making bricks to build huge cities. But the hard work didn't kill them as he had hoped. The more he persecuted them, the more they "multiplied and grew."

Pharaoh then called for the Hebrew midwives to kill all the males who were born. He appointed two women—Shiphrah and Puah—to oversee an organized effort to make sure that the baby boys were killed at birth. These midwives, however, did not do as they were told. "And the midwives said to Pharaoh, 'Because the Hebrew women are not as the Egyptian women; for they are vigorous, and they give birth before the midwife can get to them'" (1:19). This may have been partially true and partially false. Although God does not approve of lying, these women were blessed of God because they refused to obey the evil king.

Frustrated, Pharaoh decreed that the Egyptians themselves were to throw the male children into the river. The text does not tell us that this actually happened, though it probably did. Just think of the weeping, the sorrow and terror that the Israelites experienced in Egypt!

But God had not forgotten His people. A man by the name of Amram was married to a woman named Jochebed. They had two children; and when a third was born to them, they were confronted with the cruel edict of Pharaoh. For three months they hid the child but knew that if he were heard crying, an Egyptian could throw him into the river.

If Moses was to be thrown into the river, his parents wanted to be the ones to do it! They put him into a small ark and gently left it to float at the edge of the Nile. He was in the river, just as the king commanded.

In all probability, it was Hatshepsut, the famous daughter of Thutmose I (ruled 1525–1512 B.C.), who spotted the baby Moses in the ark of bulrushes. Through a providential meeting, God put two things together: a crying baby and a woman's heart. It was one thing for the princess to hear of the decree while living in the palace, it was quite another to actually hear a crying infant and contemplate the horror of having him drown. Moses' sister Miriam was standing by and suggested that a nurse be found for the child. The princess agreed;

and of course Miriam got their own mother Jochebed to take care of the little boy.

This ordinary child would become a link in a long chain of events that would eventually lead to the nation's deliverance. The Israelites might have thought that God had forgotten them, but His providential hand was orchestrating a plan that would be worked out right on schedule.

Later, Moses is taken to the court and adopted by Pharaoh's daughter. In what has to be one of the greatest examples of divine providence, the very man who will some-day deliver Israel from the hand of a cruel Pharaoh is trained by Egyptian royalty. Later, after forty depressing years in the desert, he returns to be perhaps one of the greatest leaders the world has ever known.

I'm told that under the snow in January, God is already at work making changes in flower buds and in the roots of trees to prepare them for the warmth of May and June. God was working, even when the Egyptians were sweating under the cruel hand of a vengeful king. The invisible hand became visible in God's good time.

Moses has a message for us: *Getting closer to God should be our single motivating passion.* God's interaction with us is personal, long-term, and life-changing. Our mistakes, failures, and successes—all of these are designed to help us get closer to Him, to know Him better, and to walk in His presence with a more steady step.

We might envy Moses who spoke "face to face with God," but we have the same privileges as he. We might not hide in a cave and see God's glory pass by, but in Christ we stand in the presence of the Almighty "unveiled," speaking directly to our Lord. In an era of grace, the privileges of Moses become those of the most humble Christian.

In *Getting Closer to God* I try to begin where all of us are and, through the life of another, lead us to where we should be. God invites us to draw near, to come into His throne room and speak to Him as Moses did. If this book helps whet our appetite for more of the Almighty, it will have fulfilled its purpose.

Join me as we take some giant steps in His direction.

ONE

Life in the Penalty Box

(Read Exodus 2)

One day I received this letter:

> I am a man thirty-one years old and divorced, though I fought the divorce bitterly.
>
> I feel bad because I have no hope for the future; often I go home from church and cry. But there is no one to hold me when I cry. No one cares. What hurts most is that I've begged God for the grace to be single for His glory and to fix my eyes on Jesus, but nothing changes. I continue to fail.
>
> I am a basket case emotionally, or on the verge of collapse. Something is very wrong. I'm so crippled and embittered that I can scarcely relate to others anymore. *I feel I have to sit out the rest of my life in the penalty box.*

The penalty box—have you been there? You want to get closer to God, but He seems to hide His face. You are trying to find some purpose in your pain but there are few (if any) answers. The more you try to read the fine print of God's will the more mysterious it becomes.

Maybe it's a result of a bankruptcy you couldn't avoid, an ugly habit that brought health problems, or a past immoral relationship that keeps getting in the way of your genuine desire to make things right. Or perhaps you were unjustly fired from your job. Whatever the cause, you feel as if you are in the penalty box, much like a hockey player who has to be out of the game for a rule infraction or flagrant misconduct.

You've got a friend in Moses. He spent forty years in Pharaoh's court, another forty leading the Israelites out of Egypt, but sandwiched in between he spent another forty years in the penalty box for manslaughter. What he didn't know was that this was to be his training ground for greater things. He would eventually get close to God, but it would take awhile.

Stephen tells us in Acts 7 that Moses "was educated in all the learning of the Egyptians, and he was a man of power in words and deeds" (v. 22). He had studied mathematics, astronomy, and chemistry, as well as hieroglyphics. The son of Pharaoh's daughter, he enjoyed celebrity status and had every luxury Egypt could offer. F.B. Meyer speculates, that "If he rode forth into the streets, it would be in a princely equipage, amid the cries of, 'Bow the knee.' If he floated on the Nile, it would be in a golden barge, amid the strains of voluptuous music" (*Moses* [Grand Rapids, Mich.: Zondervan], 21).

Josephus says that when the Ethiopians successfully invaded Egypt, Moses was put in charge of the royal troops. He defeated the enemy and returned with spoils of victory. As Meyer says, the cream of Egypt was poured into his cup.

Yet, although Moses was educated as an Egyptian, he remained an Israelite in his heart. Grief gripped him when he saw his people making bricks in the hot sun. This child of luxury and fashion could have stayed in the palace, but he chose to take long walks to inspect what was happening out in the fields. The mistreatment of his people made him deeply angry.

He knew he was called to be their deliverer. His mother had shared with him how God had preserved him in a basket along the Nile. What is more, he felt the compulsion of leadership. He could not rid himself of the impression that his destiny did not lie in the palace but in taking the risk of freeing his people. The special privileges he had were not to be wasted. He was a man of destiny.

Moses might have simply used his influence to convince Pharaoh to lighten up on his persecution of the Hebrews. He might have reasoned that he could do more for them if he stayed in the palace than if he went with them into the fields. But his heart was pulsating with the burning desire to throw his lot in with them—body, soul, and spirit. "By faith, Moses, when he had grown up, refused to be called the son of Pharaoh's daughter; choosing rather to endure ill-treatment with the people of God, than to enjoy the passing pleasures of sin; considering the reproach of Christ greater riches than the treasures of Egypt; for he was looking to the reward" (Heb 11:24-26).

Only in recent years have archeologists unearthed the buried treasures of Egypt; now we are better able to understand the wealth and luxury that Moses left behind: piles of gold, art treasures, and jewels of every description. To leave the palace and opt for the fields was an incredible sacrifice. He was willing to relinquish respect and honor for contempt and hatred.

His decision was made when the pleasures of sin seemed most alluring. He had grown up surrounded by the indulgences of Pharaoh, who by now was probably Thutmose III. Moses knew all this could already be his, and there was more to come when he came into his inheritance. If he had waited to ascend the throne, he would have become the chief Egyptian god, enjoying the worship of the nation. The lap of luxury beckoned him. Resolutely, Moses said no to everything the average person would have said yes to.

One day as he walked in the fields and saw the sun-blackened bodies working hurriedly to make bricks, he saw an Egyptian whipping an Israelite. This was too much; the time for swift action had arrived. As Don Baker put it, "Moses forgot that he was Moses. He forgot that he was the prince of Egypt, the Pharaoh-elect, the yet-to-be-appointed king. In a moment of unbridled rage he struck the unsuspecting Egyptian and then wrapped his strong right arm around the overseer's neck" *(The God of Second Chances* [Wheaton, Ill.: Victor, 1991], 33). As the man's lifeless body slumped to the ground, Moses knew he had killed a man. He hid the warm but lifeless corpse in the sand (Ex 2:12).

The next day he went out to settle a quarrel among two Israelites only to have the offender say to him, "Who made you a prince or a judge over us? Are you intending to kill me, as you killed the Egyptian?" (v. 14). Moses was surprised that someone had been watching the whole ordeal. Though he had scanned the horizon carefully, apparently he wasn't careful enough. Or else he hadn't covered the corpse with enough sand. God, of course, was also watching.

What hurt most deeply is that his own people had rejected him. Stephen comments, "And he supposed that his brethren understood that God was granting them deliverance through him; but they did not understand" (Acts 7:25). He had *supposed* his people would understand! This was an unfortunate assumption. As hundreds of people who have failed in life have had to learn, it's often presumptuous to suppose that God's people will understand.

Pharaoh felt betrayed by the one who had grown up under his tutelage, so he wanted Moses dead. The Israelites would likely not have protected Moses even if they could have, so he had few options. In order to save his life, he fled to the desert.

To be hated by Pharaoh was understandable, but to be rejected by the people he had risked his life to help caused a wound that would take years to heal. He felt betrayed by his own people; worse, he undoubtedly also felt betrayed by the God whom he thought would bless him for his willingness to risk all he had for the sake of his people.

"By faith Moses ... refused to be called the son of Pharaoh's daughter," the author of Hebrews tells us. He had gone in faith to help his people, believing that God would vindicate his heroic decision. But though he did what he thought God wanted, he was brought to failure and humiliation. Either he had misread God's will or God simply was not worthy of his trust.

When he got to Midian Moses was exhausted, so he sat down beside a well. He had a box of medals; he was qualified to be the king of Egypt, but back home his reputation was forever ruined. Undoubtedly, Pharaoh let the people know that his adopted son had become a traitor.

Why had all this happened to Moses?

In the desert Moses would have time to heal. He would also have time to get to know God. Though he did not understand why his attempt at obedience had backfired, he would eventually be confronted by the God whose will now seemed so obscure. God would become Moses' teacher. Hidden away from the trappings of luxury and power, Moses would be slowly remade. His heart would be prepared for knowing the Almighty and eventually he would get closer to Him than any other man on earth ever could.

God would use the desert to teach Moses what the palace

could never have taught him. He got his education in the court of the king, but wisdom and character would be formed in the desert. What God would do *in* Moses while he waited would be just as important as what He would do *through* Moses when he acted.

What to Moses seemed to be the end of a meaningful life would actually be the beginning of one of the most celebrated careers in history. In the desert he would eventually be confronted by the God of his fathers. He would meet the "God of the Second Chance."

What lessons did Moses learn in the desert that he could not have learned in the palace?

The Lesson of Servanthood

Moses probably had never helped water sheep before, but that day, sitting under the blistering desert sun, he had his first opportunity to really serve. When the daughters of the priest of Midian came to the well, Moses protected them from rough shepherds and helped them draw water (Ex 2:16-17). Though he had been trained for more prestigious responsibilities, he did whatever he could to help. The change was beginning to happen.

When Reuel, the father of the young women, asked who had helped them, they knew only that they had met an Egyptian. "An Egyptian delivered us from the hand of the shepherds; and what is more, he even drew the water for us and watered the flock" (v. 19). They had no idea that they were in the presence of greatness. The man who had instant recognition in Egypt had now withdrawn to live in obscurity and humiliation. He was invited to Reuel's home and married Zipporah, one of the man's daughters. And from then on he was a shepherd.

Moses was now miles from Egypt socially as well as geographically. Shepherds were an abomination to the Egyptians. For forty years he did what he had formerly been taught to despise. Now this prestigious child of fame and fortune would waste his life doing what the most unlettered slave could do. He never did feel at home in the desert; he was like the proverbial square peg in a round hole. His aptitude lay in one direction, his responsibilities in another. His training appeared wasted. When his wife bore him a son, they named him Gershom, which means foreigner (v. 22). He would always think of himself as an alien, a man without a country.

As far as Moses was concerned, he expected to stay in the penalty box in Midian for the rest of his life. No one would ever be impressed with his credentials; he had nothing to do but contemplate his mistake and reflect on how badly he had been treated. In the backside of the desert, nobody cared. There were no promotions. At best he would graduate from one flock of sheep to another.

During those heady days in Egypt, mothers had undoubtedly pointed to Moses and said to their sons, "There's Moses ... be like him!" But here, no one admired his education or leadership. He knew that back in Egypt stories about his life in the palace would be erased from the Egyptian records. He was doomed to obscurity. The boredom of it all took its toll.

Though we can't say for sure, Moses likely began to spend more time with God. He might well have been put off by the mysterious ways of the Almighty, but he was intrigued by the thought that God did have a purpose for his nation, the chosen sons of Abraham, Isaac, and Jacob. He had time to remember, time to reflect, and time to pray.

Francis Schaeffer said that there are no big people and no little people as far as God is concerned, only consecrated and unconsecrated people. That's why our vocation isn't as important to God as it is to us. Moses had to learn that there can be fulfillment even in obscurity. Yes, even when we are asked to do a job for which we are not suited, it can have meaning if we do it for God.

Time goes more quickly when we serve with a right attitude! When Jacob went to work for Laban, he agreed to serve seven years for Rachel. The text says, "So Jacob served seven years for Rachel and they seemed to him but a few days because of his love for her" (Gn 29:20). The speed with which time moves depends on the person with whom it is spent.

Servanthood is best learned in the desert. It happens when we are asked to do those things for which we are overqualified. Moses had to learn it's not *what* you do but *why* you do it that matters to God. God wants our hearts, not just our hands.

Though Moses still felt far from God, his heart was opening to the possibility of knowing the Almighty. With nothing to see east, west, north, and south, he found himself looking upward. Perhaps he was beginning to realize that he was closer to God as a servant in the desert than he would have been as a ruler in the palace.

The Lesson of Trust

Moses had to learn that God is working even when He is silent, even when we cannot detect His movements. "Now it came about in the course of those many days that the king of Egypt died. And the sons of Israel sighed because of the bondage, and they cried out; and their cry for help because of their bondage rose up to God" (Ex 2:23). In the course of many days, God began to work—14,600 days to be precise! It took forty years, but God began to answer His people's prayer.

We read, "So God heard their groaning; and God remembered His covenant with Abraham, Isaac, and Jacob. And God saw the sons of Israel, and God took notice of them" (vv. 24-25).

Three verbs describe what God was doing while Moses was going nowhere in the desert. God *heard* the groaning of His people. He wasn't deaf after all. Though He didn't respond to His people's cries immediately, He was listening.

Next, God *remembered* His covenant. Though we may forget promises or even fail to deliver on those we remember, God is never careless with His commitments. For Him time does not erase details; everything is fresh in His memory. He remembers a thousand years ago with the same clarity that He remembers yesterday.

One reason why we can forget the injustices done against us is because God remembers them—and since He is the judge, there is really no reason for us to have to remember them too! Moses was learning that even when life is slow and God is silent, He is moving events along according to His timetable.

God also *saw* the needs of His people. He felt their hurts. Their ways were not hidden from Him, though deliverance was long in coming. For the moment, Moses had to learn to trust God even when He appeared to be indifferent regarding the needs of His people.

Of course, it's easy to trust God when the bush is burning,

the waters are parting, and the mountains are shaking—it's those silent years that are discouraging. But *blessed is the person who does not interpret the silence of God as the indifference of God!*

Yes, it's easy to talk about faith when you're healthy and the boss has just promoted you. When you are happy with your work and your children are following the Lord, trust comes easily. But when you've been misunderstood, misrepresented, and when you're in a job that is not suited to your abilities or training—when you've got medical bills, and an impossible marriage partner—that's when trust means most to God. *It's in the desert and not in the palace that God finds out the depths of our yieldedness.* It's when He is silent, not when He speaks, that our faith is precious in His sight.

Moses was learning that we can draw near to God even when He is silent. Faith opens the door to His presence.

The Lesson of Obedience

As we shall see in the next chapter, God came to Moses in the burning bush with an invitation to be a leader, a powerful man back in Egypt again. The time had come to get out of the penalty box and back into the game. But Moses objected, saying, "Who am I, that I should go to Pharaoh, and that I should bring the sons of Israel out of Egypt?" (3:11).

Moses was a different man. Forty years before, he had thought he could pull off the Exodus in his own strength, but now he had learned his lesson. We might expect him to say to God, "Where have *You* been? I've been just waiting to return to Egypt!" But he asked the question that anyone who has been broken by God would ask: "Who am I, that I should go to Pharaoh, and that I should bring the sons of Israel out of Egypt?"

And yet we will learn in the next chapter that Moses' question was not so much motivated by humility as it was by a stubborn refusal to say yes to the divine call. He had not forgotten what had happened in Egypt forty years ago. He was still hurting, and besides, he now had a wife and family. Returning to Egypt at this stage of his life was not a simple matter.

The desert experience convinced Moses that he could not be a leader of his people on his own, but it did not yet bring him to the point of complete surrender. Perhaps Moses even preferred by now that his people would rot in Egypt! When you're in the penalty box, it's easy to become bitter, determined to never get back into the game. Moses did not want to be hurt a second time, so he asked, "What if they will not believe me, or listen to what I say? For they may say, 'The Lord has not appeared to you'" (4:1). How did God answer this objection? He asked, "'What is that in your hand?' And he said, 'A staff'" (v. 2). Then God empowered Moses to do special miracles with it. When he threw it on the ground, it became a serpent; but when he stretched out his hand and caught its tail, it was transformed back into a staff. And when he put his hand in his bosom and pulled it out it was leprous, white as snow. But when he put it back in his bosom, it was restored.

Where did Moses get this staff, this rod with which he would do miracles? He got it when he was serving in the penalty box. Later he would stretch out his rod over the sea and the waters would part. That stout piece of wood, about five feet long, would be a constant reminder to Moses that God would be with him all the way. From then on, Moses carried this rod with him and it was used by God in defeating the Egyptians. The rod of Moses became the rod of God.

A.W. Tozer has said that the best leaders are not those who want the job but those who are conscripted by God for leadership. If Moses had a hankering for greatness, it was laid to rest in the desert. Now in the presence of the Lord he struggled, unsure of his own gifts and abilities. Yet for all of his doubts and reluctance he was at last qualified for leadership. God found it easier to use a faltering man with doubts than an eager man brimming with independence and self-will.

Moses learned, as all of us must, that we draw closer to God only because God takes the initiative to come to us. "How blessed is the one whom Thou dost choose, and bring near to Thee, to dwell in Thy courts; we will be satisfied with the goodness of Thy house, Thy holy temple" (Ps 65:4). As the work became harder, Moses would have to draw nearer. He would eventually know God in ways that no other man would.

You and Your Desert

Today, God asks you and me, "What is in *your* hand? What have you learned while on the sidelines?" Patience? Faith? The ability to love the unlovable? Have you learned to be content in obscurity? To trust God in adversity? Has shame brought bitterness or brokenness? David, who spent his share of time recouping from failure said, "The sacrifices of God are a broken spirit: a broken and a contrite heart, O God, Thou wilt not despise" (Ps 51:17).

We all have to die to what is pleasant and attractive; we have to die to the easy path that we might have the courage to choose the dangerous one. F.B. Meyer wrote that we must be

> Buried to bear fruit; maimed to enter life; laying our Isaac on the altar, to become the leader of the faithful; turning aside from the age of a sunlit garden to take the darker, stonier path; renouncing what others hold without rebuke, because of some high purpose which has forced its way into the soul; choosing Gethsemane and Calvary and the grave, in fellowship with the Man of Sorrows; being willing to renounce friends, wealth, reputation, and success, and to be found like a shipwrecked sailor on some lone shore, because of some vision that beckons us *(Moses* [Grand Rapids, Mich.: Zondervan], 23).

A pastor fell into the sin of immorality. When his sin became known, his reputation was ruined, his career seemingly over. He found a job in a warehouse, an occupation for which he was, to put it mildly, overqualified. Only a few Christian friends stood by him through the experience. No one dared recommend him to another church, though he had repented. Gifted, educated, qualified for ministry, he was now a nobody, rejected and obscure. He could have become bitter, but he began to serve God where he was. He began attending a church—first as a visitor, then as a member, and within time he became a Sunday School teacher. He was faithful in what he did, spending much time being quiet before God.

A year went by, then another. God began to give him greater ability, more opportunities. "God loves to hurt His people," he would say. "The branch that feels the sharp cut of the pruning knife eventually bears fruit." Today this man is out of the penalty box and has an effective ministry.

Not every story, of course, has such a happy ending. But if we learn our lessons in the desert, we'll find it's not really a penalty box at all—it's really God's training ground for a deeper, less self-centered ministry. There is a new touch of God that comes in the desert.

Three years after I received the letter from the man who complained about having to spend the rest of His life in the penalty box, I received this encouraging letter from him:

I am writing to testify of the marvelous grace of God. I've learned many lessons in my desert—my penalty box—but God has used my pain to bring me lovingly, mercifully to Him.

Just when I thought I was hopeless, God revealed my sin and self-centeredness that was my sad condition before Him. He stripped me of my pretensions and showed me my unbelief. I learned that God cannot simply be one of my options, but I must risk my life, my soul, my sanity on Him, and Him only. I must believe that He is exactly who He says He is in His Word. When I was most bankrupt, He gave me the strength to forsake all and follow Christ.

Before, my focus was always on me: my happiness, my circumstances, my emotions. Now, it is on God. As a by-product of focusing on Him, His joy is alive in me. Though tough circumstances still have their sting, I can cast my care on Him and He gives me "His exceeding great and precious promises."

It strikes me that these are admonitions I have heard for years, but it is the *doing* of them that makes all the difference.

During my desert times, false cults and false brethren

would offer a way that seemed right, but would cast doubt upon the Word of God. Yet, I found victory by fully committing myself to God. Thank God, I'm out of the penalty box and back in the game.

Moses had to learn that God delights in making servants, not Pharaohs. And He can do His best work in obscurity, not in the limelight. God would rather that we get closer to Him than fulfill our most fond wishes. He will leave us in the desert until we hear His voice and seek Him with a single motive.

Don't let Satan talk you into wasting your failures. God is with you in the penalty box to teach you to serve, trust, and obey. Eventually you may even get to play in the game again.

Moses did not know he had been in training. Getting closer to God, he learned, may be more important than becoming the star player on the team. To be sidelined is not a waste of time if you get private tutoring from the Coach.

But there was so much more to learn.

TWO

Excuses! Excuses!

(Read Exodus 3–4)

Left to ourselves we would never seek for God. But God graciously comes seeking for us, prompting us to do His will, and giving us the courage to respond. When He draws near, we are tempted to back off. Obedience to what we know God wants us to do is seldom easy.

To the darkness God said, "Let there be light!" And there was light.

To the storm Christ said, "Peace, be still!" And there was a great calm.

To a great fish the Lord said, "Swallow Jonah!" And the sea monster obeyed.

We, however, think we have the power (if not the right) to defy divine commands. We can dig our heels in and confidently proclaim, "I won't!" And we don't. For a short time. And to our own detriment.

Moses himself stood toe to toe with God, arguing about the job description he was personally handed in the desert. In the end he acquiesced to the great I AM, but it was a stretch.

Moses, as we have learned, spent forty years in the palace as a *scholar*. Then he spent another forty years in the desert as a *shepherd*. Now at the age of eighty he had come to terms with the disappointment of the past. He did not know that he would spend the next forty years becoming a *savior* to the nation of Israel. He would not go down in history as a Pharaoh, but as a prophet.

While near Mount Horeb in the Sinai range, Moses turned to see a strange sight: A small acacia bush was on fire and it kept burning without being consumed. Strange indeed. "And the angel of the Lord appeared to him in a blazing fire from the midst of a bush; and he looked, and behold, the bush was burning with fire, yet the bush was not consumed. So Moses said, 'I must turn aside now, and see this marvelous sight, why the bush is not burned up'" (Ex 3:2-3).

What began as a remarkable sight turned out to be a spectacular miracle. The bush kept burning long after the branches would normally have been consumed. "When the Lord saw that he turned aside to look, God called to him from the midst of the bush, and said, 'Moses, Moses!' And he said, 'Here I am'" (v. 4). Moses had heard his name!

Then the Lord said, "Do not come near here; remove your sandals from your feet, for the place on which you are standing is holy ground" (v. 5). The Lord then identified Himself as the God of Abraham, Isaac, and Jacob. And incredibly, the Lord told Moses that He had now come to intervene in the plight of His people, the Israelites, and that Moses was chosen to return to Egypt to lead the people to the Promised Land!

What an honor!

God could have delivered the people Himself by a series of creative miracles. He could have assigned the task to angels or He could have chosen someone who had a better track record in the eyes of both the Egyptians and the Israelites. Instead, He chose to use an imperfect person to do a great task on earth. But for now, Moses was not impressed. He did not want to have a part in the divine action.

We might expect him to exclaim, "Yes, Lord! Whatever You say!" But he tried to weasel out of God's call. Just like many of us, he protested, hoping to persuade God to change His mind.

Forty years ago he had run ahead of God, but he now lags behind. He had tried to rescue the people alone and failed, but now he shrinks back from delivering the people even if God should help him. No matter how spectacular the burning bush, no matter how startling to hear his own name, Moses was in no mood to return to the very place where he had failed.

So he objected, offering five excuses for disobedience. Rather than getting closer to God, Moses wanted to get away from Him, or at least get away from this divine call. Incredibly, he did his best to defy the call of God while standing barefoot on holy ground! Right there in the presence of the Almighty, *standing on a place sanctified by divine fire, Moses objected to what God wanted him to do!*

We can come to church, sing the right hymns, and recite orthodox prayers while disagreeing with the God we profess to love. Even a sanctuary dedicated to God can be the place where we disregard the call of the Almighty. Neither our geographical location nor our physical posture is proof of obedience. Only when we say yes in our hearts is God pleased.

What excuses did Moses offer? Without taking time to think, five desperate pleas came immediately to mind. Out of the abundance of the heart the mouth speaketh. We just might hear ourselves in his objections.

Here are his excuses.

"I'm Not Adequate. I'm a Nobody!"

"Who am I that I should go to Pharaoh, and that I should bring the sons of Israel out of Egypt?" (3:11). Moses saw himself as inadequate for the job—just like when we are asked to teach a Sunday School class or to share the gospel with a friend, and are tempted to say, "I'm not a Luther or a Calvin or a Billy Graham ... who am I that I should do this?"

Moses might not have realized that he had posed the philosophical question of the ages. Our culture is particularly obsessed with the question, "Who am I?" Husbands have left their wives to find out who they are. Mothers have left their children to establish their own identity. We just don't seem to know who we are.

Walk into any Christian bookstore and you will find dozens of books on the general topic of developing a healthy self-image. We are told that people must have a good opinion of themselves; they have to know how special they really are. We should be glad that Moses asked God this question so that we can better understand the Lord's opinion of the psychological dimensions of our self-perception.

Incredibly, God ignored Moses' question. He simply gave a promise: "Certainly I will be with you, and this shall be the sign to you that it is I who have sent you: when you have brought the people out of Egypt, you shall worship God at this mountain" (v. 12). How will this help Moses know who he is?

The answer to the question of who Moses was, was found in knowing who God was! Only when we are rightly related to God can we establish that sense of identity, that healthy self-image. We do not improve our self-image by thinking better of ourselves, but by thinking rightly about the God who loves us and honors us with His promises.

Moses' question was not a sign of humility. He was speaking with a tone of self-deprecation that revealed his own lack of faith and willing obedience. Humility means that I see my weakness; it also means, however, that I see God's strength. Behind Moses' question was stubborn unbelief.

God's promise should have been enough to compensate for

Moses' sense of inferiority. Though he did not feel up to the job, he could rely on the abiding presence of God. If there was a need for wisdom, God would give it; if there was a need for power, God had an unlimited supply. God would be his senior partner and companion. God was not so much calling Moses to go to Egypt as He was calling this discouraged shepherd to Himself.

Today we can count on the same promise. We need not be distressed about our financial future nor should we be overcome with fear about those who want to do us harm. "Let your character be free from the love of money, being content with what you have; for He Himself has said, 'I will never desert you, nor will I ever forsake you,' so that we confidently say, 'The Lord is my helper, I will not be afraid. What shall man do to me?'" (Heb 13:5-6).

God has the right to lead us precisely because He has the ability to help us. The Almighty would stand beside Moses every moment of the day. The abiding presence of God is all that Moses could have asked for.

Is Moses satisfied? Is he content, knowing that God will not tie him to a branch and let him blow in the wind? No, Moses has a second excuse.

His problem is deeper.

"I Don't Know Enough"

"Behold, I am going to the sons of Israel, and I shall say to them, 'The God of your fathers has sent me to you.' Now they may say to me, 'What is His name?' What shall I say to them?" (Ex 3:13).

Moses fears he will be asked questions for which he does not have an answer. If he doesn't even know God's name, how will he handle the inevitable doubts that the people will have? And, is it not presumptuous to assume that the one and only true God sent him?

God answers this objection by telling Moses that He is the great I AM. Specifically He says, "'I AM WHO I AM'; and He said, 'Thus you shall say to the sons of Israel, "I AM has sent me to you"'" (v. 14). Literally this phrase means, "I exist because I exist." God is the self-existent One. He is the one uncaused being in the universe. He gives account to no one.

Moses will now be able to give an answer to those who ask about his authority; he will be able to say that he is coming as a representative of the self-existent God. The God of Abraham, Isaac, and Jacob will authenticate Moses' new career. Moses has all he could ask for.

We've all experienced the same fear, haven't we? We have kept our mouths shut about our faith because we fear people will ask, "How do *you* know?" Our response should be to point to the credentials of Christ, and affirm that we do not speak on our own behalf. We are not simply giving our opinion about the big questions of life. We speak on behalf of someone who claims to be God and has the credentials to prove it.

After the first objection Moses was given an answer for his weakness: God Himself would be with him. Now he also has an answer for his lack of knowledge and authority: God Himself will assume the responsibility of proving to others that Moses represents the self-existent One. God knew Moses' name; Moses is now given God's name. But Moses is still not ready to pack his bags and leave for Egypt.

He has yet a deeper problem.

"I'll Be Rejected"

"What if they will not believe me, or listen to what I say? For they may say, 'The Lord has not appeared to you'" (4:1).

For forty years Moses had been nursing his hurt, the pain of rejection. The day he defended one of his own brothers from the hand of an Egyptian he knew he was making a clean break with Pharaoh's court. He expected the people to recognize him as their deliverer. Instead, he was humiliated, stung by those who should have rallied to his cause. He was banished to the desert. He does not want to risk a replay.

God graciously gives Moses three signs to silence the skeptics. His rod, when thrown on the ground, would become a serpent; his hand, when put in his bosom, would become leprous; and if he were to fill a bucket of water from the Nile and pour it on the ground, it would become blood (vv. 2-9). In other words it will be up to God, not Moses, to convince the people that what he had to say was coming from a higher authority.

These miracles would prove to be greater than those performed by the skilled pagan magicians. The people would be convinced that Moses was indeed sent by God.

What more could Moses ask for? He had the promise of God's presence, the assurance of God's own name, and now miraculous credentials that would convince his cynical people that returning to Egypt was not his idea but God's. And yet Moses is not ready to return.

He had an even deeper problem.

"I Don't Have Any Natural Talent"

"Then Moses said to the Lord, 'Please, Lord, I have never been eloquent, neither recently nor in time past, nor since Thou hast spoken to Thy servant; for I am slow of speech and slow of tongue'" (v. 10).

"God, You are calling someone for a responsibility You have not equipped him to do! I lack the ability!"

Evidently Moses stuttered or at least found that his speaking was slow and difficult. He imagined himself entering the palace, walking up the long corridor and standing before Pharaoh surrounded by a legion of his soldiers. And after appropriate protocol, he could see himself beginning to make the unthinkable request for the Israelites to leave the land, only to find no words coming out of his mouth.

Or what if he spoke so slowly, belaboring every word, that he would elicit the ridicule of the court? How could he be God's spokesman if he was not good at speaking? It would make sense that a spokesman for God should be gifted in speech!

God's reply is enough to silence the objection of any person who thinks that his or her physical handicaps are limitations to God. "And the Lord said to him, 'Who has made man's mouth? Or who makes him dumb or deaf, or seeing or blind? Is it not I, the Lord?'" (v. 11).

God's surprising answer? Deformities are made by God! If God wanted Moses to have an eloquent tongue, the Almighty would have given him one. God takes responsibility for creating the person with one talent just as much as He takes responsibility for creating the person with ten. We are given enough abilities to do whatever God calls us to do. Evidently God thought that Moses' speech impediment would not stand in the way of success in Egypt. So what if God chose to let Moses begin his next forty years with what Don Baker calls "a humbling limitation"?

At last, we think, Moses would have his objections answered. He is going under the auspices of the Creator God in whose hands all things rested. We expect him to say, *yes!*

Yet, the problem evidently is still deeper.

"I Don't Want to Go"

Finally, Moses reveals his heart. "Please, Lord, now send the message by whomever Thou wilt" (v. 13). Lord, if it's absolutely necessary I'll go, but can't You find somebody else?

Moses' answer is a grudging acceptance of God's will, but it also exposes what lay behind all of his excuses. He simply did not want to go. Surely there was another leader with better qualifications who would take this responsibility.

His objections cloaked a fundamental desire not to have his nest disturbed. He didn't like the price tag of obedience. Beneath the surface was a root of stubbornness, a hardness that had developed in his old age.

No matter how much Moses hated Midian, the thought of going to Egypt was worse. He had come to terms with the endless monotony and humiliating task of caring for sheep. He was in a vocation where failure was, for all practical purposes, impossible.

Egypt represented risk. Speaking on behalf of God and for an entire nation was frightening. Continual rejection was a distinct possibility. So was an untimely death at the hands of an irritated king. Life in the desert had not been pleasant, but it looked so much better than an unpredictable, highly visible career in Egypt.

He also had a wife and children to think about. Would they come with him to Egypt or stay with his in-laws? And what if the old wounds were reopened? He had tried, after all, to unite the nation against the cruel policies of a past Pharaoh. He could still taste the gall of the rejection he had suffered as a result. The present with its misery was safer than a risky future played out at great personal cost. The ghost of past failure had not been put to rest.

If he had to go, he would. But if God were merciful, He would send someone else to complete this assignment. Yes, God had an answer for his excuses, but what remedy was there for his stubborn heart? Even after his reluctant yes, Moses hoped that the Almighty would change His mind.

God was not amused. "Then the anger of the Lord burned against Moses, and He said, 'Is there not your brother Aaron the Levite? I know that he speaks fluently. And moreover, behold, he is coming out to meet you; when he sees you, he will be glad in his heart.... Moreover, he shall speak for you to the people; and it shall come about that he shall be as a mouth for you, and you shall be as God to him'" (vv. 14, 16). If Moses thought he wasn't gifted in speech, he could rely on his brother Aaron who was still living in Egypt. This was not ideal, but at least he had a spokesman.

Moses departed and returned to his father-in-law and asked permission to leave for Egypt. He took his wife and sons and put them on donkeys and began the trek back to the land of his youth. And of course, he also took his staff with him, the rod he had used while doing time in the desert.

He left not knowing what awaited him. He knew the task wouldn't be easy, for God told him that Pharaoh's heart would be hardened so that he would not let the people go. Since the Almighty had not changed *His* mind, Moses would have to do the best he could.

Think of what Moses would have missed if he had not gone back to Egypt! Yes, he would not have had to put up with a disgruntled, stubborn nation that grumbled with every step taken in the desert. But he would also have missed the humiliation of the gods of Egypt, and the incredible victory of crossing the Red Sea. More important, he would have missed forty days of uninterrupted fellowship with God on Mount Sinai, and would not have stood with the Lord fourteen hundred years later on the Mount of Transfiguration. While Moses was running for cover behind a canopy of excuses, all of these honors (humanly speaking) hung in the balance.

Moses can be grateful that God prevailed. To this day the nation of Israel is grateful that God prevailed. The angels are grateful that God prevailed. We are grateful that God prevailed. Only Satan is angry.

Our Excuses

Moses represents us all. We have all defied God at one time or another. We do it every time we make a home in our hearts for sin and compromise with the world. When we cheat to get ahead, when we manipulate our circumstances according to our liking, we disobey God. And when we turn away from known guidance, we defy the Almighty.

Some of us have known exactly how God was leading us

either to become a missionary or to leave our present vocation for another. Yet we have argued, resisting the changes that obedience would bring. Or we hang on to the sin which so easily entangles us.

If the truth were known, it is not because "there are hypocrites in the church" that a man turns away from Christ. Nor is it because "there are so many different interpretations of the Bible" or because "it isn't fair for God to accept only one religion when there are so many in the world." As the saying goes, when we are convinced against our will, we are of the same opinion still.

Former first lady Nancy Reagan said that as a boy her father attended Sunday school and memorized some verses in a contest to win a new Bible. But the pastor's son, who didn't recite the passages as well as he, wound up with the prize. And though her father died at the age of eighty-four, he never forgot the unfair treatment he received at the age of ten. He never attended church again.

A hundred excuses may be given for ignoring the claims of Christ. We can think of endless reasons why we might say no to God's persistent call on our lives. But behind the facade is a fundamental unwillingness to be disturbed, a determination that our foundations will not be shaken, a stubborn disposition that does not want God to rule our lives.

Moses teaches us that when we *excuse* ourselves, we *accuse* ourselves. Our excuses reveal our hidden fearful disobedience. Even a flimsy excuse can be used to protect an unwilling heart.

Ron Hutchcraft tells of walking with a missionary through a jungle in Central America. When they came to a clearing, there was a river that could only be crossed by walking on a pipe that had been laid across the rushing water. The missionary was accustomed to crossing, but Ron struggled, wondering if there was not a better way. He says, "I had come as far as I could safely.... If I was to continue, I would have to leave my comfort zone and take a risk!"

Playing the game safely can take us only so far. Often God brings us to a place where we have to leave the familiar for the unfamiliar; we have to be pushed out of our comfort zone and take a risk. *God loves to lead his people in places where they have never been before.*

When Queen Elizabeth was crowned in 1952, those of noble blood received invitations with the words, "All excuses set apart." It was unthinkable that someone would have used an excuse to miss the coronation!

When the King of Kings calls us to come beyond the boundaries of our safety zone, every excuse must vanish. Standing on holy ground, we cannot argue with the One whose promises are with us and whose Spirit indwells us.

When God closes in, we must let Him draw us nearer to His heart. Obedience opens the door to deepening our relationship with Him. Nothing will make us get closer to God than being forced to walk in unfamiliar territory.

After a testy time with God, Moses was on his way.

THREE

The Mystery of God's Ways

(Read Exodus 4:18–5:23)

"Can you say that you really know God?"

That's the question I asked a Jewish lady who was sitting next to me during a recent plane trip. We had chatted about her background, her moral convictions, and her commitment to the religious life of the synagogue. But I needed to understand where she was on her spiritual journey.

"No," she said, "I can't say that I know God ... in fact, I'm not sure that God can be known; He seems to be too obscure."

I found myself both agreeing and disagreeing with her. God is often obscure and difficult to understand. But He can be known; we can say, yes, we know Him. Just because we can't know everything about God does not mean we cannot know *something* about Him. And more than that, we can communicate with Him.

When the Prophet Daniel described the turbulence of the last days as the forces of Antichrist grow in power, he wrote, "But the people who know their God will display strength and take action" (Dn 11:32). The people who know their God will not buckle under the pressure.

George Mueller, you might recall, believed that the first duty of every Christian was to have his soul "happy in God." Those who are happy in God can survive even when there is not much else to be happy about. They have an inner

43

contentment that does not fluctuate with the harsh realities of personal existence. Moses had to draw near to God; and when life became difficult, he was pushed nearer still.

After Moses reluctantly agreed to go to Egypt, he had three experiences that forced him to rethink his view of God. The better Moses knew the Lord the more likely he would be able to resist the temptation to run and hide when Pharaoh would unleash his anger against him. When we fear only God we need never fear man.

Three encounters introduce Moses to three of God's attributes—*sovereignty, holiness,* and *faithfulness.* He emerges with a deepened understanding of God's ways. The mystery of God will always puzzle him, but the better he knows God the more intrigued he will be. Rather than running away from the Almighty, he will seek Him out. And as he gets closer to God, he will gain a clearer picture of how to interpret the events that will unfold in Egypt. Moses' education in the ways of God began almost immediately after he agreed to return to lead the nation out of their distress.

The Sovereignty of God

When he was still in Midian, God gave Moses these startling words: "When you go back to Egypt see that you perform before Pharaoh all the wonders which I have put in your power; but I will harden his heart so that he will not let the people go" (Ex 4:21). God, Moses had to learn, is sovereign in history.

Why would God harden Pharaoh's heart? And how could God hold Pharaoh responsible for his behavior if he was just following the script God had written? These are questions which have been debated for centuries, but the bottom line is that such acts are consistent with the character of God.

Many Bible teachers say that Pharaoh hardened his heart first and therefore God had a right to harden it at a later time. But that is not quite fair to the text, for already in Midian, before Moses arrived in Egypt the Lord said, "I will harden his heart so that he will not let the people go." God promised He would do this before the request even reached Pharaoh's desk.

Even if Pharaoh hardened his heart first, we are still faced with the question of why God would make Pharaoh's hard heart even harder. Why would God harden a man's heart under any condition? Would we not expect God to always soften hearts rather than harden them? What about free will?

To begin with, we must realize that God might have hardened Pharaoh's heart simply by withdrawing common grace. By abandoning Pharaoh to his own rebellion, the heart of the king would become more deeply entrenched against God. Or perhaps God gave Satan permission to enter Pharaoh so that he would be more adamantly set against the Almighty.

But—and this is important—even if God only *permitted* Pharaoh's heart to be hardened, God still is the one who hardened the king's heart. After all, He could have chosen to not permit the hardening of Pharaoh's heart. Therefore, the hard heart of a king, like all other events in the world, must be understood as a part of divine providence. Whatever God permits, He ordains.

Second, if we ask whether God has the right to harden a man's heart (as explained above), the obvious answer is yes, of course. If God hardens a man's heart, he must have the right to do it. God is sovereign over His creation. He can do as He wishes with His creation.

Most people believe in "the freedom of the will," but the Bible teaches that the human will is, by nature, controlled by sin. When the humanist Erasmus wrote a book defending the freedom of the will, Luther replied with a full-length book titled, *The Bondage of the Will.* He says that the will may be likened to a beast. When this beast is ridden by God, it goes where God directs it; when it is ridden by Satan it goes where Satan directs it. The will is not exactly "free"; it is influenced by other causes.

Luther, unlike modern men, was not interested in the question, *Who* am I? but rather in the question, *Whose* am I? If we belong to the devil, we do his work; if we belong to God, we do *His* work. We may perceive that our will is free, but it is also subject to sin, Satan, and God. "The king's heart is like channels of water in the hand of the Lord; He turns it wherever He wishes" (Prv 21:1).

This does not mean that we are passive pawns, waiting for God to free us from our satanic deceptions. Satan works, but so does God. We must be warned, however, that if the Almighty gives us the desire to seek Him we must respond, so that He might deliver us from our delusions. The same God who hardened Pharaoh's heart draws the hearts of so many others to Himself.

Paul asked whether there is injustice with God, since He deals with people according to His will. His answer: "May it never be!" (Rom 9:14). Then comes the clincher: "For the Scripture says to Pharaoh, 'For this very purpose I raised you up, to demonstrate My power in you, and that My name might be proclaimed throughout the whole earth.' So then He has mercy on whom He desires, and He hardens whom He desires" (vv. 17-18).

Paul anticipates our objection.

You will say to me then, "Why does He still find fault? For who resists His will?" On the contrary, who are you, O man, who answers back to God? The thing molded will not say to the molder, "Why did you make me like this," will it? Or does not the potter have a right over the clay, to make from the same lump one vessel for honorable use, and another for common use? What if God, although willing to demonstrate His wrath and to make His power known, endured with much patience vessels of wrath prepared for destruction? (vv. 19-22)

Paul politely tells us to mind our own business, since we have no right to pry into God's secret counsels!

God wanted to use Pharaoh to display His power. This pagan king would persist in strident opposition, so that God would need to do signs and wonders to overpower him. This would be an example of what happens when a self-willed, proud, and determined man stands in opposition to God. In the end Pharaoh would be humiliated and God glorified.

Why did God share this bit of theology with Moses? Obviously, Moses could have met with Pharaoh without knowing that his hard heart was a part of the plan of God. Yet the Almighty graciously gave Moses this insight for a very good reason: *Moses would be encouraged to know that the resistance he was to encounter was a part of God's providential plan.* No matter how powerful Pharaoh appeared to be, this pagan king was in the hands of the Almighty. No stubborn heart can stand in the way of God's ultimate blueprint. Indeed, stubborn hearts are used by the Almighty to display His power and fulfill His will.

If we struggle with God's sovereign justice, we can rejoice in His sovereign mercy. Immediately after God's word about Pharaoh, Moses was told, "Then you shall say to Pharaoh, 'Thus says the Lord, Israel is My son, My firstborn'" (Ex 4:22). Though God took Pharaoh's hard heart and made it even harder, He overcame the blindness of Israel's heart by choosing Abraham and his descendants for special blessing. As Paul wrote, "So then He has mercy on whom He desires, and He hardens whom He desires" (Rom 9:18).

If you are plagued today by the question of whether you have been chosen by God; if you wonder whether you are a Pharaoh or an Abraham, let me assure you that there is only one way to find out: Come to Christ in humility and repentance and receive His promise that you will not be cast out. As the writer of Hebrews states, "Today if you hear His voice, do not harden your hearts" (Heb 3:7). If we have the desire to pursue God, we should do so.

Yes, God is sovereign even over the human heart. Moses should go to Egypt with the confidence of knowing that the coming obstacles were not simply foreknown by the Almighty, but were actually ordained by Him. *Moses was to be comforted, not confused, by the divine use of power.*

Perhaps you are working or living with people who are particularly stubborn, who resist rational dialogue. We must understand that the providence of God extends even to the human will, and that He will use such people for His own glory. Such an understanding of the sovereignty of God enables us to cope with the perplexities of human conflict.

As Moses pondered these words he knew that he would encounter an angry Pharaoh, but he also knew that he had believed in a God who would triumph. God would raise up an obstruction simply to prove that there was no obstacle He could not overcome!

Moses was getting closer to God.

The Holiness of God

Moses and his wife Zipporah and their children expected that they would have a peaceful journey to Egypt, a respite before the conflict would begin. But when they chose to spend the night at an inn, Moses was smitten with illness and his life was in jeopardy.

Moses almost died because he had overlooked one of the commandments of the Lord:

> Now it came about at the lodging place on the way that the Lord met him and sought to put him to death. Then Zipporah took a flint and cut off her son's foreskin and threw it at Moses' feet, and she said, "You are indeed a bridegroom of blood to me." So He let him alone. At that time she said, "You are a bridegroom of blood"—because of the circumcision.
>
> EXODUS 4:24-26

What was this all about?

Moses had not followed God's instructions that his son be circumcised. Evidently, he had neglected this because his wife was opposed to what she thought was a disgusting, bloody act. While Moses is lying ill, smitten by God, she performs the rite of circumcision and throws the foreskin at the feet of her sick husband exclaiming, "You are indeed a bridegroom of blood to me!"

Moses had to learn that God expected obedience even if a commandment was unpleasant and painful. He was the head of his home and should have insisted on doing what was right even if his wife objected. If he were to be an example to the people, he had to get his own house in order. *To lead a nation, he had to lead his home.*

Many men disqualify themselves for spiritual leadership because they do not give leadership to their families. Perhaps a man has a wife who does not want to attend church or who is of a different faith, so to maintain peace he backs away from his God-given responsibilities. Obedience in family matters calls for both sensitivity and strength.

Of course the tables are often reversed. Frequently the wife is the one who has deep spiritual commitment and is forced into taking the role of leadership because of a disinterested or hostile husband. Even so, in the day of reckoning, the man will be held accountable.

Moses might have protested, arguing that his judgment was more severe than he deserved. He might have pointed out that he was already showing obedience by returning to Egypt. Was this really the way he should be treated? God was, however, teaching him that those who are called to lead must be obedient; in fact, they especially must be careful to do as God commands. The greater the responsibility of leadership, the greater the discipline for disobedience.

Obedience to one command did not absolve Moses from obedience to another. The question was not whether the matter of circumcision was big or little, but whether it had been carried out according to God's command. Even keeping the peace at home is never an excuse for disobedience.

Years later Moses would be forced to obey God almost

singlehandedly. While much of the nation sank into idolatry and even his older brother Aaron joined in the fray, Moses would have to stand alone, calling the nation to repentance. No doubt he often remembered that night in the inn where he almost died because he had taken a casual attitude toward God's instructions.

With his life hanging by a thread, Moses had learned a second powerful theological lesson: God is holy and will not overlook a trespass no matter how reasonable the infraction may appear to us.

The holiness of God both attracts us and repels us. We are drawn to worship God for His holiness; but without His grace and mercy, we would shrink away in fear, guilt, and shame. Every man who has a glimpse of God is smitten by his own sinfulness.

Moses was severely disciplined, but he was also encouraged to draw near, to learn more about the God who accompanied him en route to Egypt. His knowledge of God was growing, and with each encounter he was more convinced that God was to be both loved and feared.

After arriving in Egypt, he would get a further glimpse of God and be encouraged. There was another reason to trust in God.

The Faithfulness of God

Moses returned to Egypt and was able to have an audience with Pharaoh. He would not have been able to enter the presence of the king if he had not been remembered as the man who had grown up in the previous king's court. The new king probably heard from his advisers that a request for a meeting had come from a man who himself was once in line to be Pharaoh. He also was likely told that this man had betrayed his legacy by turning against the king and siding with the Jewish slaves.

Think of the memories Moses must have had as he walked up the long corridor and approached the reigning Pharaoh! As a child he had run through those hallways, and as an adult he had strutted past the historical monuments with a strange mixture of awe and disgust. At the age of forty, he had been tempted to opt for the treasures of Egypt, but his conscience would not let him.

Now at the age of eighty he stood before the king as a representative of a God he had only recently come to know. "Thus says the Lord, the God of Israel, 'Let My people go that they may celebrate a feast to Me in the wilderness'" (Ex 5:1). The ultimate intention was that Israel leave permanently, but God wanted to prove that the Pharaoh would not even accept a reasonable request for a short retreat.

Moses knew what was coming: "Who is the Lord that I should obey His voice to let Israel go? I do not know the Lord, and besides, I will not let Israel go" (v. 2). The request was impertinent. Why should Pharaoh respond to the petition of another god when his own had served him so well?

The angry king interpreted the request as nothing more than a diversionary tactic. The sons of Israel were his slaves, directed to build cities such as Pithom and Ramses. They served the noble purpose of contributing to the glorious buildings of Egypt. But if the people had nothing better to do than request a leave, it was positive proof that they were too idle.

So Pharaoh met with his taskmasters, those who directed the Israelite foremen responsible for the building projects on a day-to-day basis. He issued this command: "You are no longer to give the people straw to make brick as previously; let them go and gather straw for themselves" (v. 7). That in itself might have seemed reasonable, but it was coupled with the demand that the quota of bricks they made was to remain the same!

Moses' confrontation with Pharaoh was a disaster. When the taskmasters emerged, they relayed the message to Israel's foremen and to Moses and Aaron, who were waiting just outside Pharaoh's court. When the Israelites heard the terrible news, they blamed Moses: "May the Lord look upon you and judge you, for you have made us odious in Pharaoh's sight and in the sight of his servants, to put a sword in their hand to kill us" (v. 21).

The next morning the slaves had to begin work much earlier, cover more territory, and yet make the same quota of bricks. If they didn't do so, they were beaten. "Let the labor be heavier on the men, and let them work at it that they may pay no attention to false words" (v. 9). And when the foremen of Israel formed a delegation to go to Pharaoh, he accused them of being lazy. "You are lazy, very lazy; therefore you say, 'Let us go and sacrifice to the Lord'" (v. 17).

Stand for a moment in Moses' sandals. You didn't want this job in the first place. You had told the Lord why you were ill-suited for this leadership role. You had become content in the desert. If it lacked excitement, at least it also lacked criticism. Reluctantly you have done your best and now you are blamed for making a bad situation worse.

Moses chose his only reasonable option. He cried to God, "O, Lord, why hast Thou brought harm to this people? Why didst Thou ever send me? Ever since I came to Pharaoh to speak in Thy name, he has done harm to this people; and Thou hast not delivered Thy people at all" (v. 22).

Moses had been introduced to God's sovereignty and holi-

ness, now he needed the encouragement of His *faithfulness*.
The Lord graciously reveals the meaning of His name to Moses
and then reaffirms His promises:

> God spoke further to Moses and said to him, "I am the
> Lord; and I appeared to Abraham, Isaac, and Jacob, as God
> Almighty, but by My name, Lord, I did not make Myself
> known to them. And I also established My covenant with
> them, to give them the land of Canaan, the land in which
> they sojourned. And furthermore I have heard the groaning
> of the sons of Israel, because the Egyptians are holding them
> in bondage; and I have remembered My covenant. Say,
> therefore, to the sons of Israel, 'I am the Lord, and I will
> bring you out from under the burdens of the Egyptians, and
> I will deliver you from their bondage. I will also redeem you
> with an outstretched arm and with great judgments. Then I
> will take you for My people, and I will be your God; and you
> shall know that I am the Lord your God, who brought you
> out from under the burdens of the Egyptians. And I will
> bring you to the land which I swore to give to Abraham,
> Isaac, and Jacob, and I will give it to you for a possession; I
> am the Lord.'"
>
> EXODUS 6:2-8

Seven times God says, "I will." God will honor His
covenant; the pain of His people has not escaped His notice.
He will bring the people out from under the hand of Pharaoh
according to schedule. The conflict with Pharaoh is not up to
Moses to resolve. God has a plan; He has a purpose that will
be accomplished. In fact, as we have already learned, this rebellious king is a part of God's grand scheme.

Why did God say that by His name, Jehovah, He had not made Himself known to the patriarchs? (v. 3). He had used the name Jehovah when He made Himself known to Abraham, Isaac, and Jacob (e.g., Gn 13:4). Yet, the patriarchs did not know the meaning of the name Jehovah; they did not know God as the Promise Keeper, the One who personally would deliver His people. They saw God's mercy and power but did not think of God as the dependable Redeemer.

God was saying, *Moses, your obedience might have backfired, you may have your own nation angry at you, but My faithfulness will outlast this terrible blow. When you encounter temporary setbacks, you must take time to look at My long-range plans. Your friends might desert you when the going is difficult, but I will be with you no matter what.*

Moses was learning, as all of us must, that the trials of life should drive us to God's heart. If we are obstructed by stubborn people, we must learn that God uses even them to accomplish His will and purpose.

Conflicts at home or at work test our obedience to God. And when we experience the sharp knife of betrayal God will be with us, making up for the changeable nature of our fair-weather friends (Ps 73:25-26).

Pharaohs come and Pharaohs go, but God is there. Friends come and go, but God is there. A spouse might be faithful or unfaithful, but God is there. And when we are falsely accused, God stands with us through the trial. *That which is beyond our control is tightly in His grasp.*

Joni Eareckson Tada has, as of this writing, spent twenty-six years in a wheelchair as a result of being paralyzed in a diving accident. In an interview, she points out that this is a long period of time; and just when she seems to be managing it, she says she gets a new affliction that prevents her from keeping speaking commitments and deadlines. "But," she says, "God is more concerned with my growing closer to His heart than keeping commitments or public ministry."

Read her words carefully:

> It's odd, but my suffering, mostly my physical affliction—has been that which has made my quest easier. At night I have to lie down by 8:00, and all I can move is my head. And that's like fasting. My disability is a physical condition that subdues my wanton spiritual appetites. I have to go to God. I have no other place to go. So it hasn't been a roadblock on my quest for God; it has paved the way ... the only way we can enjoy heaven is to allow God to take our heart home first (Quoted in Legioner's *Conference Journal*, March 5, 1993, p. 4).

Interestingly, Joni does not say that the reason she so longs for heaven is that she might have a restored body, though she admits she looks forward to standing on her own two legs and then kneeling to worship Christ. She longs for heaven, she says, to be free from the struggles of sin she has within her mind.

In his book *Knowing God*, J.I. Packer says there are four characteristics of people who know God. They (1) have *great energy for God*. Survey church history and you will find that those who knew God stood for truth even at great personal cost. They were sensitive to situations in which God's truth and honor were being directly or tacitly jeopardized, and sought to change the situation regardless of the personal risk.

Then, (2) they have *great thoughts for God*. Daniel, who knew God, gave us some of the greatest insights regarding

God's sovereignty over the affairs of men. Those who know God are willing worshipers of the Almighty.

Those who know God, (3) show *great boldness for God.* Once Daniel and his friends were convinced that their stand was right, to quote Oswald Chambers, they "smilingly washed their hands of the consequences." Once such people believe they have found God's will, they can stand even if others do not stand with them.

Finally, (4) those who know God have *great contentment in God.* They are at peace with themselves because they are at peace with God. The weight of condemnation has been lifted, so they have inner resources to cope with disappointments.

Like Moses and Joni, we all must learn that God does not forsake us when life becomes difficult. He shows us another side of his character that will sustain us. He enlarges our understanding of His providence and power. He wants to prove that He is faithful even if He does not deliver us from our distress. He remains mysterious, but we can trust His heart.

Moses was getting closer to God than he had ever been. He knew that God was as near to him as when the bush was burning and the Angel of the Lord was speaking. He was getting to know a God he could trust.

The closer he came to God the more peacefully he could accept his humiliating defeat. A step backward was actually a step forward if God was in control.

But this was only the beginning.

FOUR

Toppling Those Idols

(Read Exodus 6–10)

"When Hitler has done his worst, we will do our best," said Winston Churchill, at a time when World War II was going badly. He knew he would have to rally the troops, keep up morale, and convince a beleaguered generation of British folks that the war could be won.

Moses, we have learned, left the palace of the king disappointed, perhaps even feeling betrayed by God. He did what was right, but his obedience backfired. And there was no easy way to fix it. When he went to the people to explain what happened, we read, "but they did not listen to Moses on account of their despondency and cruel bondage" (Ex 6:9).

His credibility was shattered. Any thought that he might look like a hero evaporated. His friends wished Moses had stayed in Midian, for his well-intended efforts had only increased their suffering. *After Moses had done his best, Pharaoh had done his worst.*

When God asked him to set up a second appointment with Pharaoh, Moses said, "Behold, the sons of Israel have not listened to me; how then will Pharaoh listen to me, for I am unskilled in speech?" (v. 12) Apparently even Pharaoh had heard that the Israelites were no longer on Moses' side. If the Israelites didn't listen to Moses, why should Pharaoh?

When God repeated the request, Moses repeated his objec-

59

tion: Pharaoh won't listen anyway (v. 30). But Moses was encouraged when God promised that the Israelites were soon to witness a contest between the Almighty and the pagan idols revered in Egypt. The lame, ineffective gods that had captured the allegiance of a nation were about to be exposed as frauds. So Moses took his brother Aaron and together they made a trip to the palace to see Pharaoh again.

Standing before Pharaoh, Moses and Aaron were requested to perform a miracle to prove their authority. In response, "Aaron threw his staff down before Pharaoh and his servants, and it became a serpent" (7:10). Although we might expect Pharaoh to be impressed, he calmly called his own magicians and evidently they performed the same miracle. There was one crucial difference, however: "But Aaron's staff swallowed up their staffs" (v. 12).

False gods attempt, as far as possible, to counterfeit what the true God is able to do. These magicians, evidently named Jannes and Jambres (2 Tm 3:8), probably used a combination of trickery and demonic power in their attempt to duplicate what God was doing. Sometimes they were successful, but most often they failed. But they gave Pharaoh the confidence he needed to tell Moses and Aaron to leave.

Moses will eventually learn that God is always at war with idolatry. Whether it is the gods of the pagan Egyptians or the gods of present-day America, God cannot tolerate competition. It's not that God is insecure about His position in the world, but it's because He is the only Being who is worthy of worship and ultimate allegiance. Our value is derived from Him, and He alone is the source of His own worth.

Moses would also learn that false gods are tolerant of one another. A culture can believe in polytheism (many gods) as long as all of those gods are finite. Egypt had many gods, at least eighty in number. Indeed, Pharaoh (likely Amenhotep II) himself was considered a god. His clothing had the symbols of deity, and he gladly received the worship of his subjects.

To make His point, God decided to make a mockery of a few of these gods and of Pharaoh himself. Some gods who had broad areas of responsibility were affected by more than one of the plagues. And because different parts of Egypt had different gods, identifying which gods corresponded to which plague is somewhat difficult. But we are not left to guess what God was up to. He said openly that he was doing this to "make a mockery of the Egyptians" and again, "against all the gods of Egypt I will execute judgments—I am the Lord" (Ex 12:12). The stage was set for a classic struggle between God and His would-be rivals.

Come with me on a quick tour of several chapters of Exodus, and let's imagine what Moses was thinking when he saw the power of God on display. He saw the battle between two wills—the will of a powerful and rebellious king and the will of a sovereign God. Moses was learning that the idolatry men love so much, God hates so passionately.

These nine plagues are all different but serve the same end. Together they give us insight into God's divine purposes. At the end of this chapter, I will summarize the new understanding Moses had about God. Day by day Moses was getting closer to the heart of the Almighty.

The Nile Turned to Blood

God told Moses to tell Aaron to stretch out his staff over the rivers and streams, and they turned to blood in the very presence of Pharaoh and his advisers. By now Moses' faith had grown to the point where he actually believed the miracle would happen, and it did. The fish died and the stench throughout the land was unbearable.

This was a judgment on Apis, the bull god of the Nile, and Isis, the goddess of the Nile. These gods were worshiped because the Nile River was crucial to the life of Egypt.

Again the magicians and sorcerers appeared to duplicate the miracle. Since the whole Nile was already blood, they couldn't redo that spectacle, but perhaps they took water from a well and made it appear red like blood. Whatever, it was enough to convince Pharaoh that he had no reason for concern. He hardened his heart and wouldn't let the people go.

Pharaoh didn't back down, but neither did God.

Frogs Appear

Frogs were sacred to the goddess Heqet and were regarded as emblems of fertility. Now this god, instead of being a help, became the object of hatred. Frogs crunched under the feet of the Egyptians. They got tangled in the dough as the women kneaded bread. They croaked from cupboards and closets.

This second miracle was also repeated by Pharaoh's magicians. We might well doubt whether these sorcerers had the ability to create life (such is likely a prerogative of God alone). But through trickery they made it appear as if they were able to cause frogs to multiply just as Moses had done. But when Pharaoh wanted the frogs removed, he had to call on Moses to do it! His magicians had failed him. In frustration Pharaoh called Moses and said, "Entreat the Lord that He remove the frogs from me and from my people; and I will let the people go, that they may sacrifice to the Lord" (8:8).

Had Pharaoh finally been convinced of the superiority of the Lord? Was he finally ready to let the people go?

Hardly.

Moses prayed, the frogs died, and Pharaoh changed his mind!

Lice Cover the Land

The god of the desert was named Set, and he had responsibility for protecting the land from an invasion of insects. Now with a stroke of his rod, Aaron turned the dust of the earth into gnats (lice) that swarmed throughout the region. The presence of these pests humiliated everyone.

Pharaoh was losing some confidence in his magicians, but gave them an opportunity to prove that they were equal to Moses and Aaron. This time, however, they admitted that they simply could not duplicate the miracle and confessed, "This is the finger of God" (v. 19).

Pharaoh, however, was too stubborn to budge. Just as God had predicted, he hardened his heart and would not let the people go. More insects were on the way.

Flies Swarm

Re, the god of the sun, was represented by the fly. Now suddenly there were swarms of these insects that covered the ground and came into the houses of the people. The devastation was so complete that the whole land was "laid waste" with the pests.

Evidently, the first three plagues had come to the whole land, including the territory of the Israelites. But beginning with the swarms of flies, God made a division between the two parts of the country and protected the Hebrews from this judgment (v. 23).

In desperation Pharaoh called Moses and made the first of three compromises. He said the Hebrews could worship in the land (v. 25). He pressured Moses to accept partial obedience as sufficient to satisfy the request of the Lord.

Moses pointed out that it would be an offense to sacrifice sheep in the land since the Egyptians considered these animals to be an abomination. The nation would have to leave in honor of the word of the Lord.

Pharaoh did not argue the point, but suggested a second compromise, "You may sacrifice, but don't go far away" (v. 28). He even adds, "Make supplication for me."

Is Pharaoh beginning to soften his stance? Is this the beginning of what Moses sought—permission to leave?

Moses took Pharaoh's word at face value and prayed to God and the swarm of insects disappeared. Any hint that Pharaoh was beginning to soften quickly vanished, however, once the crisis was over. Not everyone who nods in God's direction is ready to make a complete surrender.

Pharaoh took a walk under the clear sky and his heart became hard. He stubbornly refused to let the people go.

Disease to Domesticated Animals

The next plague made a mockery of Hathor, a goddess with a cow's head, and Apis the bull god, a symbol of fertility. The horses, donkeys, camels, herds, and flocks of the Egyptians died. Apparently it affected only animals that were "in the field" (9:3). This explains why some cattle were still alive when the plague of boils came a few days later.

Despite this blow to the Egyptians, the animals of the sons of Israel were unharmed. When Pharaoh sent his men to investigate this strange phenomenon, he was angry and again hardened his heart. He was more determined than ever not to let the Israelites go.

The Plague of Boils

Sekhmet, the goddess with power over disease, was severely humiliated when the next plague arrived. Moses took fine dust and threw it into the sky. And with that, an epidemic of boils descended on both man and beast throughout the land of Egypt. The pain and itching of these ulcerated sores created a revolting spectacle. The magicians never even tried to duplicate this miracle because the boils were on them too!

Pharaoh himself, god that he was, was humiliated. But he dug in his heels, and said, "No!"

Thunder, Lightning, and Hail

Nut, the sky goddess, and Osiris, god of crops and fertility, proved powerless when this intense storm swept through the land. Trees were uprooted and the flax and barley were cut to shreds. The thunder, hail, and lightning were "very severe, such as had not been in all the land of Egypt since it became a nation" (v. 24). The blast struck the animals that were out in the field, the plants, and the trees. It incited terror in the hearts of the Egyptians.

Pharaoh finally made a confession: "I have sinned this time; the Lord is the righteous one, and I and my people are the wicked ones. Make supplication to the Lord ... and I will let you go, and you shall stay no longer" (vv. 27-28).

That certainly sounded like a conversion of some sort. So Moses walked out of the city and spread his hands to heaven. And the wind and hail stopped. At last, he had permission to leave.

Pharaoh then took another walk outside his beautiful palace. He breathed fresh air and felt the warm sun stroke his body. And he concluded that he had repented too hastily. So he repented about his repentance! The answer was still no!

The Swarm of Locusts

Nut, the sky goddess, and Osiris, god of crops and fertility, were humiliated again. When Moses predicted that locusts would come, they were on their way. Pharaoh's advisers were terrified. They called a top-level meeting and gathered the courage to tell their "god" that it was time he let the Israelites go. They asked, "Do you not realize that Egypt is destroyed?" (10:7) At least, they said, let the men go and sacrifice to their God; if the women and children stayed in the land, then the men would surely return.

Pharaoh reluctantly agreed. He brought Moses back into the palace and said that the men would be allowed to go to serve the Lord. When Moses replied that the whole nation intended to leave, Pharaoh became angry and said no.

On command, the plague of locusts swarmed throughout the land. The sun could not be seen for the clouds of these pests. This was the worst infestation of locusts recorded in history. These hungry insects ate whatever was left after the vicious hailstorm. "Thus nothing green was left on tree or plant of the fields through all the land of Egypt" (v. 15). The locusts entered the stockpiles, the houses, and undoubtedly the palace.

Pharaoh couldn't take it any longer. He hurriedly called Moses and Aaron and said, "I have sinned against the Lord your God and against you. Now therefore, please forgive my sin only this once, and make my supplication to the Lord your God, that He would only remove this death from me" (vv. 16-17).

A genuine conversion at last? Perhaps now Pharaoh is turning to God. Moses prayed and the east wind that brought the locusts stopped and a west wind came and blew them all away.

By now you have already guessed it: Pharaoh changed his mind. He hardened his heart and would not let the people go.

Darkness That Could Be Felt

The sun gods Re and Horus could do nothing when Moses stretched out his hand toward the sky and darkness settled over the land of Egypt. For three days there was no movement; each person had to remain where he was when the darkness descended.

Pharaoh made a plea bargain. During the plague of flies, he had made two compromises: (1) He said they could worship in the land; then, (2) he said they could leave but not go far away. Now, (3) he suggested that all of the people could go if their cattle and herds stayed behind. Obviously he wanted these animals to replace those that had been killed during the plagues.

Moses pointed out that they needed their animals for sacrifices. No person nor beast should be left behind.

Pharaoh refused and told Moses to leave and never return. "'Get away from me! Beware, do not see my face again, for in the day you see my face you shall die!' And Moses said, 'You are right; I shall never see your face again!'" (10:28-29) With that, the king sealed his own doom.

The more often Pharaoh broke his promise the harder his heart became. Eventually, God would win the tug of war, and Pharaoh would die angry and defiant. He along with his gods would be humiliated.

The last plague was the most devastating of all: The firstborn son among all the Egyptian families died on the same night. This plague must be considered in detail in the next chapter since it became the basis for the Passover in the history of the Israelites.

The Meaning of the Plagues

It takes but a few minutes to read the description of these plagues, but let's not forget that Pharaoh and his people actually experienced them over a period of perhaps six to nine months. Moses, who was the focal point of the controversy, learned that God was to be loved and worshiped, but also feared. There was more to God than His sovereignty, holiness, and faithfulness. God was on a mission; He had a point to prove and He did it with flair and persistence.

Like a lens that is better adjusted, the plagues of Egypt brought the character of God into sharper focus. The closer Moses got to God the more he understood about the divine mind; he was learning how deeply God felt about paganism and the rebellion of an angry king.

At close range, Moses saw the *judgment* of God. These plagues had some of the characteristics of natural events, but they were not just a stroke of bad luck served up by the happenstance of nature. For one thing, they did not happen randomly, but always came and left in accordance with Moses' prayer.

Also, they were more intense than natural phenomena. Egypt has always had frogs, but not so many that they filled the people's houses. There have always been diseases among cattle or locusts in the fields, but never was the nation paralyzed by such plagues. No nation has ever had three days of "darkness that could be felt." These were natural phenomena raised to a higher power.

They also increased in intensity. The first plague was against the Nile, other plagues were against the animals, but the series ends with a dead child in every Egyptian home. Each arrow was more destructive than the one before it.

The magicians were right. This was "the finger of God." As far as we know, this was the only culture in history judged in this way. But because God hates idolatry, He will always judge this sin wherever it is found, whether the judgment takes place in this life or the one to come.

How does God judge idolatry today? He begins by bringing His own people to the point where they realize the foolishness of cavorting with idols. He causes our idols to forsake us at the time of need. He gives us despair in the place of fulfillment; trouble in the place of happiness. He has our god come down with a severe case of boils!

If your experience is like mine, fighting the idols of the heart is something like pulling up weeds in the garden. Just when you think you have them all, they sprout again. That's why the Christian life is one of continual repentance.

As for the unsaved, God will often make them dissatisfied with their idols too. He will give them a hunger for something better, and eventually some will see their need to seek God's forgiveness.

God often brings judgment to the unrepentant by abandoning them to their idols. When the tribe of Ephraim was enamored with its gods and refused the prophet's warnings, God finally said, "Ephraim is joined to idols; let him alone" (Hos 4:17). *The worst judgment is to find yourself satisfied with your idols.* He who is content with idols will never seek the true God. Only in eternity will it become clear that his gods have deceived him.

If we think God's judgment is too harsh, it might well be that our conception of idolatry is too superficial. God asks,

"To whom then will you liken Me that I should be his equal?" says the Holy One. Lift up your eyes on high and see who has created these stars, the One who leads forth their host by number, He calls them all by name; because of the greatness of His might and the strength of His power not one of them is missing.

ISAIAH 40:25-26

Understandably, idolatry is offensive to the Almighty.

Moses was also growing in his understanding of the *uniqueness* of God. There are some things that pagan gods can do. But only God can create life. Only God can take a rod and turn it into a serpent. Only God can take dust and turn it into gnats.

And only God can stop the plagues throughout the land once they have come. At best, false gods have a mixture of success and failure. Magicians and sorcerers who give themselves to Satan have the power to do some miracles, but not many.

False gods always seek to imitate the true God. Since they are woefully inferior, they attempt to counterfeit whatever God does. Satan insists he can give us everything God can without the need for humility and repentance. His aim is to give a pleasing (though deceptive) alternative to faith in the true God. He wants his followers to be satisfied customers until he has them firmly under his control.

God is special. He neither imitates other gods nor does He learn from them. He is in a class by Himself and has no serious rivals. "Remember the former things long past, for I am God, and there is no other; I am God, and there is no one like Me" (Is 46:9).

But perhaps the most striking attribute displayed in the plagues is the *jealousy* of God. Jealousy is sin for us because we have no inherent rights. For God, jealousy is right and proper: He *deserves all of the praise, honor, and worship there is in the universe.* He does not have to pass it on to a being who created Him; nor would it be right to share it with one of His creatures, since they would be receiving what they do not deserve. Idolatry violates the very nature and position of the true God.

Moses was learning that this was more than a contest to see which god is more powerful. God hates idolatry and is committed to proving that false gods cannot deliver. Even Pharaoh, the Egyptian god par excellence, was humiliated through this public contest. He was personally irritated by frogs, plagued with lice, and in pain with boils. In the end he and his armies drowned. Let the false gods do what they can, let them deceive people as often as they can, but in the end they are reduced to dust.

America today desperately needs to learn about the jealousy of God. For example, sex is one prominent god of our day. This god promises pleasure, fulfillment, and meaning. Books, magazines, and movies are committed to the idea that sex outside of a man-woman marriage relationship is not only permissible, but desirable. We have humbly bowed before this god of sensuality.

The result? God is grieved because He does not have our hearts for Himself. "Do not love the world, nor the things in the world. If anyone loves the world, the love of the Father is not in him" (1 Jn 2:15). God asks His people to give their hearts to Him with exclusivity and single-mindedness. He expects special devotion because He Himself is worthy.

Money is another god that over-promises. My wife and I met a woman who, as an owner of a hockey team, reportedly was worth about $50 million. We sat next to her during a game, and could see her wrinkled, anxious, and unhappy face. About a year later she died of cancer. Her money could not save her. Once more this god was forced to bite the dust, to admit that in the end, it was hollow and empty.

A woman whose husband has built an empire out of pornography was asked how she felt about her husband's preoccupation with other women. She replied, "How can I be critical of something that has brought me this much money?" Her god made incredible demands which she apparently was willing to pay. But the end result will be disappointment and judgment.

Another god is power. Pharaoh was the consummate "control freak" who hardened his heart, vengeful to the end. Three times he asked Moses to pray for him. Sometimes, in desperation, he prayed the prayer of a penitent. But his heart was never changed because he was not brought to the point of submission; *he bent but he never broke.*

In effect, Pharaoh experienced a whole series of deathbed conversions. He cried for help because he was in trouble, not because he saw himself as a sinner who needed God's mercy. Eventually he let the people go because he had to. His change of mind fell far short of a God-given change of heart. After the Israelites left he followed after them, hoping to bring them under his control once again. As we shall see, the reward of his stubborn efforts was to be drowned in the Red Sea.

The man who rules his family with an iron fist is also obsessed with power. So is the businessman who wins by intimidation, or the church member who must always have his way. Anything that stands in the way of complete submission to God is an idol that must be put away.

Pharaoh died, committed to his gods. But if a man does not break before God because he *wants* to, in the next life he will break because he *has* to. God will never tolerate competition for very long. The higher false gods rise, the farther they will fall.

Moses was learning that when false gods have done their worst, God will do His best. Count on it.

FIVE

Redeemed at High Cost

(Read Exodus 12)

No freedom can compare to walking away from the burdens of the past. The more painful the past, the more joy when leaving it behind. If God did not have an answer for our past, we could have no confidence for our future.

It's our privilege to relive the story of how God freed the Israelites from generations of slavery so that they could begin the trek to the Promised Land. This event was so critical that God changed the calendar, making the fourteenth of Nisan (April) the beginning of Israel's year. They would celebrate like they had never celebrated before. This would indeed be a new beginning.

The tenth plague was different from all the rest. It was the most severe, striking dead the firstborn in every home that was not prepared for the Angel of Death. Also, it would become the basis of the Passover, that ancient rite which Jews still observe today. Finally, it is the clearest picture of redemption in all of the Old Testament. Deliverance from Egypt is a picture of our deliverance from sin and Satan.

Most of us have never seen the President of the United States in person, but if we did, we would recognize him instantly. Thanks to the many pictures we've seen of him, he would be easily identified. Just so, those who understood the Passover were able to recognize Christ when He came. In this ancient ritual we see the coming Redeemer.

As for Moses, his confidence in God was growing. The first nine plagues had convinced him that his cause would eventually triumph. He was getting to know that God is a God of judgment; he had seen the *jealousy* of God in His mocking of the pagan gods. Now he needed to see the *redemption* of God. He needed to see His tender mercy, His deliverance and faithfulness.

No man can say that he knows God unless he is a student of redemption, for salvation is God at His finest (at least from our perspective). Through this door, we enter into His sacred counsels and glimpse His purposes.

We don't know how God communicated His instructions for the Passover to Moses. By now Moses easily recognized the voice of God because of either distinct impressions or actual words. The heart of God was now opened for all to see. Here are the steps the Israelites took in planning for this memorable celebration.

They Found a Perfect Lamb

The Lord spoke to Moses, "Speak to all the congregation of Israel, saying, 'On the tenth of this month they are each one to take a lamb for themselves, according to their fathers' households, a lamb for each household'" (Ex 12:3). If a lamb was too big for a household, families celebrated together so that nothing would be left over.

Not just any lamb, mind you. The lamb had to be perfect. "Your lamb shall be an unblemished male a year old; you may take it from the sheep or from the goats" (v. 5). The standard for Passover lambs is explained more fully in Leviticus 22:22-24: It could not be blind, or have a crooked nose or a broken hoof or any broken bones; it could not have any boils or scabs or scars on its skin and its wool had to be fleecy white.

Why this standard? Because the *outward perfection of the lamb was a picture of the inward perfection of our Savior.* Paul wrote that Christ "knew no sin" (2 Cor 5:21). And the author of Hebrews wrote, "For we do not have a high priest who cannot sympathize with our weaknesses, but one who has been tempted in all things as we are, yet without sin" (Heb 4:15). Peter said that Christ was the lamb without blemish and without spot. When Christ was conceived, the Angel Gabriel referred to Him as "that holy thing." Only a Savior who had triumphed over sin could lift us from our own sinful predicament.

This perfection of the lamb had to be proved over a period of time. "And you shall keep it until the fourteenth day of the same month" (Ex 12:6). Since it was selected on the tenth day, it was to be observed for four days before being killed.

For thirty years Christ was observed by His family and friends; for three years He was observed by the multitudes. Even His enemies had to admit that He was "without blemish."

Pilate said, "I find no fault in Him," and Judas later confessed, "I have betrayed innocent blood." Even the demons of hell said, "We know who You are, the Holy One of God." In order to convict Christ, His enemies had to hire liars so that He could be falsely accused and put to death. God the Father approved of Christ's perfection when He said, "This is My beloved Son, in whom I am well-pleased" (Mt 3:17).

Christ had a level of holiness that could not be seen by the human eye. He was not just sinless, but had the positive quality of righteousness that belongs only to God. As the Son of God

He was just as perfect and as righteous as His Father. This explains why we need His righteousness to be accepted by God. We become the "righteousness of God in Him" (2 Cor 5:21). We become so shrouded with His righteousness that God can see no fault in us.

David Koresh, who led eighty-five of his followers to a fiery death in Waco, Texas, claimed to be the messiah, but he admitted that he was a sinful messiah. But a sinful messiah is a useless messiah.

God accepts only a sinless messiah, and of those there is but one. As the Israelites carefully looked for a perfect lamb, they were beginning to learn about God's ways. Moses was intrigued, getting ever closer to God's heart.

They Killed the Lamb

Regarding the Passover lamb, we read, "Then the whole assembly of the congregation of Israel is to kill it at twilight" (Ex 12:6). That chosen lamb had its neck slit with a knife. As the blood gushed warm from the wound, it was caught in a basin. Neither the Passover lamb nor Christ died accidentally or of natural causes. Both were chosen to be deliberately put to death.

Though one person killed the lamb, the whole assembly gave its approval. When the religious leaders cried out, "Crucify Him! Crucify Him!" they later affirmed that they were willing to have His blood be upon them and upon their children. Peter, on the Day of Pentecost, accused the whole nation of crucifying Christ. "Therefore let all the house of Israel know for certain that God has made Him both Lord and Christ—this Jesus whom you crucified" (Acts 2:36). Both the Passover lamb and

Christ were killed by the whole assembly.

When was the lamb slain? Literally the Hebrew says, "between the evenings," which according to Jewish tradition was somewhere between three in the afternoon and six in the evening. This was the exact time of day Christ was crucified. We know that He died on the day the Passover lambs were killed (Jn 18:28). We also know that He died between three and six. "And about the ninth hour [3 P.M.] Christ cried out with a loud voice, saying 'Eli, Eli, Lama sabachthani?' that is, 'My God, My God, why hast Thou forsaken Me?'" (Mt 27:46). Some time after this He cried out, and "yielded up His spirit" (v. 50). So Christ died in the later afternoon just as the lambs throughout Jerusalem were being slain.

A third similarity: When both the Passover lamb and Christ were put to death, no bones of their bodies were broken. Christ died earlier than expected, and when the soldiers came they did not break His legs, though this was contrary to the Roman method of crucifixion (Jn 19:31-37).

So both the Passover lamb and Christ were put to death though they were perfect; both died on the same day of the year and at the same hour of the day; both had no bones broken.

To study the Passover is to look into a mirror and see the details of Christ's magnificent work on our behalf. The Israelites might not have understood it all, but they knew that they were sinners and that God was providing protection from His wrath.

They Sprinkled the Blood

"Moreover, they shall take some of the blood and put it on the two doorposts and on the lintel of the houses in which they eat it" (Ex 12:7). The reason for this was clear:

> For I will go through the land of Egypt on that night, and will strike all the firstborn in the land of Egypt, both man and beast; and against all the gods of Egypt I will execute judgments—I am the Lord. And the blood shall be a sign for you on the houses where you live; and when I see the blood I will pass over you, and no plague will befall you to destroy you when I strike the land of Egypt (vv. 12-13).

The application of blood would make a sharp distinction between Israel and Egypt. This distinction could not be taken for granted, because the Israelites would suffer the same fate as the Egyptians if they did not obey what Moses had commanded.

Blood was to be sprinkled above the door and on both side posts. Why in these three places? Perhaps this represented the cross of Christ: The lintel represented the vertical tip of the cross; the doorposts the horizontal branch. But there was no precedent for this; no scientific reason why the homes with blood on their doors would be safe. The faith of Moses had kindled faith in two million people who took their cue from him.

Only blood on the door would save them. A locked door would not keep the Angel of Death from entering. Pleading ignorance or some other reasonable excuse would not spare them. Only blood would be recognized as protection. Those who applied the blood did not have to defend themselves, for the blood spoke on their behalf.

Moses was learning that when God redeems, He does so justly. The firstborn among the Israelites were redeemed quite apart from personal merit. Those who had blood on their door were not partly saved and partly exposed to judgment. In fact, it was not even their estimation of the worth of the blood that mattered. *The value God placed on it was all that mattered.*

We can imagine a troubled firstborn asking, "Daddy, are you sure I will be saved?" The father could take him outside and point to the blood and say, "You will be safe."

The firstborn may have been a great sinner. And although it is much better to be a small sinner (as sins are judged from our perspective) rather than a great one, that night no such distinctions mattered. Indeed some of the firstborns of the Israelites may have been greater sinners than those of Egypt. The angel of the Lord made no such distinction but recognized only blood on the door. So today, God looks for the blood; without it, no small sinner can be saved; with it, no big sinner can be lost.

Or perhaps the firstborn was emotionally troubled, filled with indecision and doubt. A skeptic might have knocked on the door of the Israelite, taunting him, reminding him of his past failures, proving that he was just as great a sinner as an Egyptian firstborn. How could the boy (or his father) respond to such accusations? He need not have given any defense; he could have simply admitted his sin and then pointed to the blood on the door.

Some families may have been so sensitive that they thought fresh blood was disgusting. They preferred a practical form of religion: Prayers, generosity, and good deeds. This list might have been tacked to their door, reminding the Angel of Death that they were too good to be judged. Nevertheless the firstborn would have been smitten. No substitutes for blood were accepted.

Again, another family may have argued that they should be spared because they were admirers of the lamb. But even if they kept the animal in their back yard, proving their devotion to it, they would have died. Millions today admire Christ but they will not be saved. To esteem Christ as a mighty teacher and an example of love will not keep us from God's judgment. God had spoken. Blood on the door was all that mattered.

That morning a loud cry swept throughout the land as the Egyptians shared their grief. Just as Moses had predicted, those families that did not have blood on their doors mourned the death of their firstborn. The nation was united in its grief. "And Pharaoh arose in the night, he and all his servants and all the Egyptians; and there was a great cry in Egypt, for there was no home where there was not someone dead" (Ex 12:30).

We may not understand why blood is important to God, but it is. Blood is not only necessary when we initially believe in Christ, it is also the basis for continued fellowship: "But if we walk in the light as He Himself is in the light, we have fellowship with one another, and the blood of Jesus His Son cleanses us from all sin" (1 Jn 1:7). More of that later.

They Feasted on the Lamb

After the blood was sprinkled, the Israelites were to roast the lamb and eat it that very evening (Ex 12:8). While Egyptian sons were *dying*, they were to be *dining*. Think of the contrast: Egypt is preparing for *funerals*, the Israelites are preparing for *feasts*. Egypt is experiencing *judgment*, Israel is experiencing *joy*.

Why should they eat the lamb whose blood had saved them? The lamb was the main dish of this meal, satisfying their physical appetite. The lamb that saves is also the lamb who satisfies.

Christ, who died for us, is the same Lamb whom we spiritually enjoy. Our Lord said that He was the bread from heaven, and the bread He gave us to eat was His flesh. When the Jews wondered at this statement, Christ replied:

Truly, truly, I say to you, unless you eat the flesh of the Son of Man and drink His blood, you have no life in yourselves. He who eats My flesh and drinks My blood has eternal life, and I will raise him up on the last day. For My flesh is true food, and My blood is true drink. He who eats My flesh and drinks My blood abides in Me, and I in him.

JOHN 6:53-55

Some theologians are bent on interpreting these words literally. Various theories exist as to how the elements at the Communion table turn into the literal body and blood of Christ. But Christ is speaking figuratively, because, (1) cannibalism seems inconsistent with the general teaching of the Bible; and, (2) the Old Testament forbade the drinking of blood. (3) Christ Himself explained that, "It is the Spirit who gives life; the flesh profits nothing; the words that I have spoken to you are spirit and are life" (Jn 6:63).

Christ's point is that we should enjoy Him; we should have our souls satisfied with His nourishment. We are saved through faith in His blood, but we grow through fellowship with His life. God is most glorified when we are satisfied with Him.

Along with the lamb the people ate bitter herbs, which symbolized their bondage in Egypt, and unleavened bread, which reminded them that they had to leave the land in a hurry so they did not have time to let their bread rise.

Leaven is a picture of evil because (1) it has a power that is much greater than its size. Paul asked, "Do you not know that a little leaven leavens the whole lump of dough?" (1 Cor 5:6). Even a small sin can affect our entire lives; it can defile us and many others besides. And (2) leaven spreads secretly, leavening a whole lump of dough when we cannot even see it at work.

Paul chided the believers in Corinth for failing to cast out the leaven, a reference to an immoral man who was allowed to stay in the church. "Clean out the old leaven, that you may be a new lump, just as you are in fact unleavened. For Christ our Passover also has been sacrificed" (v. 7).

Even today during the Feast of Unleavened Bread, Orthodox Jews go through their homes in a ceremonial search to find leaven, a reminder that their personal lives should be free from the corruption of sin. The unleavened bread was a metaphor for spiritual cleansing.

Meanwhile, the death in Egypt was immediate. "Now it came about at midnight that the Lord struck all the firstborn in the land of Egypt, from the firstborn of Pharaoh who sat on his throne to the firstborn of the captive who was in the dungeon, and all the firstborn of cattle" (Ex 12:29). Even Pharaoh's firstborn son, the one who was to inherit the throne, died.

Pharaoh called Moses and urged him to leave and added a request: "And bless me also" (v. 32). Previously, the Israelites had requested articles of gold, silver, and clothing from the Egyptians, and their wish was granted. This was a just payment since the Israelites had worked hard for many generations without compensation. They had "plundered the Egyptians" and now they started on their long journey on the very day God had specified.

They Walked in the Liberty of the Lamb

That night about two million people left (six hundred thousand men). They had few provisions for this journey. Yes, they had baked some bread, but how long was that going to last? What would they do when their meager supplies ran out? What about water? And clothes?

There was little they could do to prepare for this new way of life. They would enter a wilderness, forced to trust God alone for everything. They had no option but to walk by faith.

Think back to the time of your conversion. Nothing you could have done would have prepared you for this new walk with God. New converts are often afraid to leave their jobs, to leave their past associations and walk trusting God for their future. But trust Him they must.

The Israelites had no map. They didn't know that God had prepared a cloud to lead them by day and a pillar of fire by night. They couldn't see the blessings that awaited them; thankfully, they couldn't see the trials either. We don't have to know where we are going, we only have to believe that God is leading the way. We control so few events in life that it is only too obvious that our future is in the hands of someone else. It only makes sense to trust the God for whom tomorrow is not a surprise.

We are called to be pilgrims, not tourists. We don't have the time nor the inclination to wander around enjoying the trip. A pilgrim has one focus—his destination.

After the nation left Egypt, the firstborn sons who had been redeemed by blood were required to be specially consecrated to the Lord. "Sanctify to Me every firstborn, the first offspring of every womb among the sons of Israel, both of man and beast; it belongs to Me" (13:2). They had been redeemed at high cost, now they were to be given back to God.

Today, we are all firstborn sons. "For you have not received a spirit of slavery leading to fear again, but you have received a spirit of adoption as sons by which we cry out, 'Abba! Father!' (Rom 8:15) When Christ died, He was forsaken by God; He bore what we had coming to us. We should gladly be consecrated to Him.

How do we become God's sons? We apply Christ's blood by faith. We transfer our trust to Him, accepting His sacrifice on our behalf. The question is not whether our sins are big or little, the question is whether we are under the protection of Christ's blood.

And once we are saved, how do we deal with the accusations of the devil? What do we do with those sins that have been confessed but still plague the mind and conscience? Praying longer will not remove the guilt, nor will spiritual sacrifices or good deeds. The Lord doesn't say, "When I see your good works I will pass over you."

In the marketplace in Rotterdam, Holland, there used to be a house known as "The House of a Thousand Terrors." During the sixteenth century, the Dutch revolted against the rule of King Philip II of Spain. To suppress the rebellion, this cruel king sent an army, instructing them to go house to house, killing all the families inside. In this house near the market square, a family cowered, fearing the death that would most assuredly come upon them. Then the father had an idea: He would kill a lamb they owned, and put its blood at the doorway, letting the blood drip onto the steps below. When the soldiers opened the door and noticed the blood, they assumed that this family had already been slaughtered so they moved on. The family was then able to escape.

We can escape the judgment of God only through the blood of His Son. Of course we cannot literally apply His blood to our hearts, but we receive the benefits of His sacrifice through faith. That blood, once applied, is our permanent means of access into God's presence in this life, and heaven in the next. When we are awash with guilt we can rest in the fact that the blood of Christ is enough for God. Thanks to the blood, we can get as near to God as His own beloved Son.

Since therefore, brethren, we have confidence to enter the holy place by the blood of Jesus, by a new and living way which He inaugurated for us through the veil, that is, His flesh, and since we have a great priest over the house of God, let us draw near with a sincere heart in full assurance of faith, having our hearts sprinkled clean from an evil conscience and our bodies washed with pure water. Let us hold fast the confession of our hope without wavering, for He who promised is faithful.

HEBREWS 10:19-23

In Paris there is a famous painting by Zwiller called, "The First Night outside Paradise." It shows Adam and Eve driven out of the Garden of Eden, planning to spend their first night in the desert. In the distance is the figure of the angel guarding the entrance of the Garden, but Adam and Eve have their eyes fixed elsewhere: they are gazing at a faint but unmistakable cross beyond the horizon.

The cross is our only way back to paradise. Moses didn't know that God would soon be requiring many other sacrifices until the one and only sacrifice would appear. He looked forward to the cross; we look back to it. But already it was clear that forgiveness is costly.

Moses and the Israelites rejoiced that God was taking them out of Egypt, but they had no idea of what awaited them. Tomorrow would be a day of breathtaking drama. Egypt was behind them, but the Red Sea was in front of them. Only God could save them now.

For a moment it looked as if He wouldn't.

SIX

Escaping From Tight Places

(Read Exodus 14)

"The difficult we do immediately; the impossible takes a little longer!" That's a sign you may have seen in a store, garage, or print shop. Yes, the impossible does take longer—a lot longer!

Moses was learning an important lesson: *If he was willing to do what was possible, God was responsible for doing the impossible.* God never expects us to do what only He can do; but He does expect us to do what we can do.

Christ would never have expected His disciples to raise Lazarus from the dead; but He did ask them to loose Lazarus from his grave clothes once he came staggering out of the cave. He would never have expected the disciples to multiply five loaves and two fish; but He did accept a boy's lunch and ask the disciples to serve the people once the miracle was in progress.

In Egypt, several months of terrifying plagues had done their work. And when the firstborn son of every family was dead, Pharaoh finally gave his blessing for the departure of the Israelites. And this time he was serious.

Or was he?

After the Israelites had traveled for some days in a southeasterly path and camped at Etham, God asked them to turn back to camp before Pi-Hahiroth, between Migdol and the sea. This change of direction would lead Pharaoh to conclude that the

Israelites were confused. When word reached him, he surmised that they were wandering aimlessly in the land and were trapped in the wilderness.

Now that the firstborn sons of Egypt had been buried, Pharaoh reconsidered his decision to let Israel go. He thought of the economic hardship that would engulf him once the slaves were gone. He was stung by the humiliation of having to give in to their demands. Not only did he change his mind, but his servants did too. They asked, "What is this we have done, that we have let Israel go from serving us?" (Ex 14:5).

The Red Sea is literally the "Sea of Reeds." The exact route the Israelites took is debated, but it was likely what is today called Lake Balah, in the northwestern part of the Sinai Peninsula. We don't know how deep this lake was, but there was enough water to drown the Egyptians.

This triggered a final conflict that proved the mighty power of God. Let's walk through the events of the next few days taking special note of the roles Pharaoh, Moses, and God played in this high drama. And then we will see what this story has to say to us in our own predicaments.

Pharaoh Pursued God's People

Pharaoh hastily recruited his army to chase after the Israelites and retrieve them. His six hundred select chariots were readied and put in the charge of his best officers. His army was the best in the world. The Egyptians were so far advanced that they used iron for their chariots; they had sharp spears and a strong contingent of horses.

In contrast, the Israelites had no military equipment. They

had nothing more than unleavened bread in their satchels, and a few sticks they used to herd their sheep and cattle. They had neither chariots nor horses. They were helpless in the presence of their notorious enemy.

Pharaoh probably intended to terrorize the whole congregation by killing some of the Israelites and bringing the rest back to regroup for another round of slave labor. His wounded pride would have demanded no less. "Then the Egyptians chased after them with all the horses and chariots of Pharaoh, his horsemen and his army, and they overtook them camping by the sea, beside Pi-hahiroth, in front of Baal-zephon" (v. 9).

The Israelites were intimidated by this excessive use of force. As Pharaoh drew near, they looked back and saw the approaching clouds of dust and felt betrayed. They cried out to the Lord but had no confidence that He could help them. Then they turned on Moses and said to him sarcastically, "Is it because there were no graves in Egypt that you have taken us away to die in the wilderness? Why have you dealt with us in this way, bringing us out of Egypt? Is this not the word that we spoke to you in Egypt, saying, 'Leave us alone that we may serve the Egyptians'? For it would have been better for us to serve the Egyptians than to die in the wilderness" (vv. 11-12).

Fear distorted their memories. Life in Egypt had not been easy; in fact, the slavery was cruel and demeaning. Faced with this crisis, they remembered the past like they wanted it to be. Never before had they faced a predicament that was so overwhelming, and there was nothing they could do about it. Not even Egypt was like this.

We've all met Christians who are shocked when they learn this lesson: Belonging to God does not exempt us from the sufferings of life. In fact, I've met some people who say that they have had more trials since they were saved than previously. The reason is obvious: *Serving Pharaoh is sometimes easier than trying to get away from him.*

New Christians sometimes admit that they are now facing a whole series of battles they knew nothing of before their conversion. Something wonderful has happened to them and the enemy does not like it. This is especially true of those who were trapped in false cults, or those who were of particular help to Satan's cause. No matter how terrible the bondage was, the fear of trying to get free is even more terrifying. Pharaoh never lets his servants go without a struggle. You may be a victim in Egypt, but even that may seem better than trying to be a free man in Canaan.

When you serve the devil, you are exempt from some conflicts because you are in league with him. As long as you are an obedient slave, doing whatever your desires dictate, the battle appears manageable. When you take the time to reflect, you realize that serving Satan is a no-win situation. He keeps demanding more while he pays you less; you always keep making more concessions until you are broken down by his cruel control. He is only temporarily appeased. Yet as bad as the situation is, it might for a time get even worse when you make a move to be free. Take a step from under his control and he flies into a rage.

The dust of Pharaoh's chariots eclipsed the Israelites' view of God. That cloud of dust seemed greater than the cloud of glory that accompanied the nation. This situation called for the extraordinary intervention of God.

Moses Believed God's Promises

Pity Moses! How would you like to have two million people angry with you? Two million fingers all pointing in the same direction. Moses was in a tight place, a wonderful place to show character, grace, and faith. A place where God alone could rescue him.

When we are in a corner, our heart is exposed. Our greatest temptation is to find an escape hatch, the nearest available exit that will appear to get us out of our dilemma. Often such an exit is created by Satan, who wants us to sin rather than trust God. The Pharaoh of our souls offers an easy way with a deadly trap skillfully hidden.

What options do we have when we are in a tight place? There are dozens of attractive but deadly escape routes. Perhaps we think we can lie our way out of the difficulty. Cheating on an exam, falsifying an application or a resumé—all of these become a possible means of escape.

A couple I know chose to live together before they were married in order to save money—one apartment is cheaper than two. That was their response to economic hardship. Abortion is a popular means of escape for a burdensome moral situation.

Even adultery can appear to be an escape from a difficult dilemma. A Chicago newspaper carried a story about a couple who borrowed $150,000 for a business venture that went sour. The man to whom they owed the money began to blackmail them since he was privy to other damaging information about the couple's business venture. Then the associate made a deal: If he could spend the weekend with this man's wife, the huge financial debt would be canceled.

Though they were appalled at the thought, they eventually

gave in. "I'll just give him my body, not my heart," the woman rationalized. That was impossible, of course. After spending the weekend with the man, her marriage was so badly damaged that eventually she and her husband were divorced.

If being in a tight place reveals our character, Moses passed this test with a perfect grade. Admittedly, he had few options, but he did remember to pray rather than panic. He did remember what he had learned in the early conflicts with Pharaoh: *Situations that are out of our control are firmly in God's grasp.*

Moses and his people were trapped with the Red Sea in front of them, the mountains around them, and the strongest army on earth behind them. If he had reacted as any man might, Moses would have prepared an apology to Pharaoh, promising that he and the Israelites would be his slaves forever, if only their lives were spared. Or, he might have come apart emotionally and resigned his responsibilities.

But he reacted, not by looking ahead to the sea (wondering if he and the people could float across?), nor by looking behind to the huge cloud of dust that grew steadily closer; he looked up, to God. No matter how high the walls, or how deep the ditch, it is always possible to look up to Someone who knows everything and who can control the outcome.

No doubt Moses remembered the promises of the past. The Israelites, God had told Abraham, would be in the land of Egypt four hundred years and then they would be brought out to go into the land of Canaan. The time was up: God had to preserve His people because His reputation was at stake.

Moses also was encouraged by the promises of the present. He heard God's voice, "Why are you crying out to Me? Tell the sons of Israel to go forward. And as for you, lift up your staff and stretch out your hand over the sea and divide it, and the sons of Israel shall go through the midst of the sea on dry land" (Ex 14:15-16). God had a plan that had never even entered Moses' mind.

Several promises were clear. First, the Egyptians would be wiped out that day. The Israelites would never again have to confront Pharaoh; they would never have to look into the angry faces of his officers. Never again would they feel the pain of the lash as they baked bricks in the hot sun.

Second, God would be glorified through this event. "Then the Egyptians will know that I am the Lord, when I am honored through Pharaoh, through his chariots and his horsemen" (v. 18).

God wanted His people to have a good night's sleep before marching through the sea, so He moved the pillar of cloud from the front of the nation to the back of them to provide a shield between them and the Egyptians. The Angel of the Lord shifted from guide to guardian (v. 19). When the situation called for the impossible, God was there.

What did God ask the people to do? For now they were to be on "standby." They were to get ready to see God work as they had never seen Him work before. "But Moses said to the people, 'Do not fear! Stand by and see the salvation of the Lord which He will accomplish for you today; for the Egyptians whom you have seen today, you will never see them again forever. The Lord will fight for you while you keep silent'" (vv. 13-14).

This was not a time to run, nor a time to fight. And their mouths were to be quiet. This was not a time for screaming in terror or shouting to their friends. This was God's moment, not theirs. He had led them into a corner and it was His responsibility to find a way out. The people had done what was possible when they sprinkled the blood on their doors in Egypt; they had done what was possible when they packed for the long trip to Canaan. But there are some tight places in life, there are some difficulties that are so great, that we can do nothing at all except look up.

It appears that Moses himself cried out to the Lord longer than was necessary, "Why are you crying out to Me? Tell the sons of Israel to go forward. And as for you, lift up your staff and stretch out your hand over the sea and divide it, and the sons of Israel shall go through the midst of the sea on dry land" (vv. 15-16). There is a time to pray and a time to act.

Moses stretched out his rod over the sea—the rod he had used to herd sheep in Midian—and the miracle began to happen. A strong wind blew that night, parting the waters. Once again *the ordinary rod of Moses became the extraordinary rod of God.*

In the morning, the Israelites began the trek through the sea bed. They encountered walls of water on either side of them, but Moses gave the command to go and they obeyed. We can imagine the children scampering down the embankment, picking up stones as they ran. Older men and women walked carefully in studied disbelief. They had doubts, but the plan of God was beginning to become clear. In the distance they could see where the shore had been.

God Achieved the Victory

What did God do in response to Moses' faith? First, He *confused* the enemy. The Egyptians raced into the sea bed expecting to overtake the Israelites. But according to Psalm 77:16-20, God caused a rainstorm with lightning and thunder, and an earthquake. As the rain soaked the dry sea floor, the

Egyptian chariots began to go out of control.

God, of course, was orchestrating the whole event. "And He caused their chariot wheels to swerve, and He made them drive with difficulty; so the Egyptians said, 'Let us flee from Israel, for the Lord is fighting for them against the Egyptians...'" (Ex 14:25). In desperation they realized that this again was a contest between their own gods and the Lord of Israel.

Second, He *destroyed* the enemy. Before they could turn around, the sea closed in on them. The crashing walls of water crushed the Egyptians so that not a single soldier survived. Their bodies and pieces of the chariots were left floating along the shore. Meanwhile, the Israelites were safely on dry land.

Why did God do this? "Nevertheless He saved them for the sake of His name, That He might make His power known. Thus He rebuked the Red Sea and it dried up; and He led them through the deeps as through the wilderness" (Ps 106:8-9). In those turbulent hours of confusion and distress, the Egyptians finally knew that Jehovah was God. Too bad that they came to this conclusion too late for it to be of personal benefit. But God received glory by humiliating their gods and proving that He has no rivals.

God also did this for the Israelites so that they would have a song to sing. There is no song that is as beautiful as a song of fresh deliverance. Not only did they sing it; but someday in heaven we will all sing the song of Moses and of the Lamb. God was glorified through His chosen friends. He was also glorified through the destruction of His enemies.

Finally, God did this to preserve His own integrity. His enemies saw His power and justice; His chosen friends saw His love and faithfulness. And to this day, we all marvel at the wonder of God's plan.

You and Your Tight Place

What does all of this mean for us today? The unchangeable God bridges the gap between Israel's experience and ours. We may never see God work as dramatically as He did back then, but He works just as surely, just as faithfully. Today we can rest on these promises.

First, God leads us into tight places. I've emphasized that the Israelites were in this predicament by the will of God. This is where the pillar of fire had taken them. The zigzags in the wilderness were divinely directed.

Living with difficulties does not mean that we are out of the will of God. A young woman accepted a job, confident that God had led her to this opportunity. Yet within three months she discovered that she was expected to make a few minor compromises for her company. She asked, "How could God have led me here?" I believe she was led to accept that opportunity so that she might be tested to see whether she would follow the Lord fully or not.

Just because your investment went sour, or just because you are having conflict in your marriage doesn't mean that you are not being led by God. The Lord sometimes leads us down a path filled with potholes, detours, and barricades. He wants to see what is in our heart; He also wants to prove Himself faithful. There are many tight places for us, but these are not tight places for Him.

What if we are in a mess of our own making? Sometimes it is more difficult to trust God when we are in a corner that we ourselves have built. What about the teenager who gets pregnant or the man who is caught cheating on his income tax? What about the woman who has been lying to her husband about an affair she is having with his best friend? Those entanglements are our own fault. We were not led into them by God but by our own rebellion.

O what a tangled web we weave
When first we practice to deceive.

Sir Walter Scott

In despair some turn to alcohol, drugs, or wanton pleasure. But these exits are delusions that only compound the initial problem. Far from providing a way of escape, these outlets only make our bondage a notch tighter, and we are pushed further into a corner. Every sinful escape is a trap that ensnares us.

We've all met people who have made wrong choices at every fork in the road. After a while, the wanderer becomes confused and despairs of finding the way back. Satan's intention is to get people to make such a heavy investment in his false ways of escape that they will despair of hope. They have walked so many miles from the main path without a map that they don't know which direction they are going, much less where the roads are. So they plunge ahead, hoping that some day they will find a path that actually leads somewhere.

When we are in a mess we ourselves have created we must learn a second lesson: *In every tight place, God provides a way of escape.* Yes, even in predicaments that are our fault, God stands ready to help us. "No temptation has overtaken you but such as is common to man; and God is faithful, who will not allow you to be tempted beyond what you are able, but with the temptation will provide the way of escape also, that you may be able to endure it" (1 Cor 10:13).

What is God's way of escape? It is to give us the grace to do what is right and live with the consequences. We might not be snatched out of our predicament, but God walks with us through it. He does not promise that we will be exempt from the fire, only that we will not be alone when we feel the heat of the flames. God will probably not drown our Pharaoh, but He will foil his attempts to bring us back into slavery.

No matter what mess you are in, there is one right decision you can still make. What that decision is might not be clear; nor is it always easy. Seek God and a trusted counselor to find a series of steps that will help you find firm footing. When we can't go to the right or to the left, like Moses we can still look up to find the wisdom we need.

How do you recognize a right decision? Often it is the most difficult one. It might be breaking a sinful relationship or apologizing to your wife or husband. It might mean that you come clean on a matter that you have been hiding for years. We must begin by giving our mess over to God and seeking His leading from there. It is never too late to do what is right.

Often we know exactly what God wants us to do, but we are confused; this confusion is often used as an excuse to find an easier way out. God's way of escape always begins with our willingness to trust His leading no matter the cost.

If you are standing at the banks of your own Red Sea, realize this: *God is just as able to help you in a predicament of your own making as He is to help you in a predicament that He led you into!* Even our disobedience, properly speaking, does not tie God's hands.

When Adam and Eve sinned, God was ready to redeem. When David committed adultery and murder, God was ready to forgive. When Daniel faced the lions' den, God was beside him. And when we cry to Him in our predicament, His ears are tuned to our prayers. Someone has said, "You can't say, 'Jesus is all I need' until you can say, 'Jesus is all I have.'"

Third, *our tight places must become God's tight places.* Even with his back to the wall, or more accurately his back to the Egyptians and his face toward deep water, there was one thing Moses could do: He was able to affirm the promises of God and put his rod over the sea. He was able to ask the people to inch forward, at least until they touched the water. He knew where the possible ended and where the impossible began.

God does not expect us to bear impossible burdens. I spoke to a young man who wanted to be a doctor but was not able to keep his grades up; the competition was just too much. I said, "Why don't you give the whole matter to God and tell Him that you're willing to accept rejection from medical school if it is His will." He replied, "I can't leave the matter entirely with God. He might not want me to be a doctor."

He had an unclear understanding of his part and God's part. His part was to work as hard as he could; God's part was to make the decision whether he should become eligible for a career in medicine. God often does not help us as long as we are still confident we can handle the matter ourselves.

What Red Sea faces you tomorrow? What Pharaoh is breathing down your neck, intending to ensnare you? What mountains do you see as you look to your left and to your right? God created the Red Sea that stares you in the face. He created the Pharaoh who seeks to enslave you. The mountains on your right and on your left are there by divine appointment. Your enemies have been raised up by God so that He might declare His power and that His name might be proclaimed throughout all the earth.

Sometimes God lets us stand on the banks of the Red Sea for

a long time; He lets us choke on the dust of the Pharaoh who seeks to destroy us. He puts us in a narrow box so that we cannot take a single step. But He has not forgotten us. He will deliver us when it pleases Him.

One day somewhere in the Sinai peninsula a tree grew. After many years it had branches that were so strong that a man chopped one off to use it as a shepherd's staff. Moses used that rod for forty years in the wilderness until God invested it with new significance. This was the rod that turned into a serpent. This was the rod that struck the earth and the dust was turned into insects. And this was the rod that Moses now held over the sea, both to open the waters for his people and to close the waters over his enemies. This rod never dreamed that some day it would play a part in one of the greatest miracles that ever took place on Planet Earth.

As Moses held the rod in his hand, so God in turn held Moses in His hand. The power was neither in the rod nor in Moses, but in God who held them both. *Every situation that is out of our hands is in His.*

Back in 1895, Andrew Murray in England was suffering from a terrible backache, the result of a long-standing injury. One morning while in his room, his hostess told him that a woman had come to the door in great distress, wondering if he had any advice for her. Murray handed her a paper he had just written, and said, "Give her the advice I have just written for myself." This is what it said:

In the time of trouble say, "First, He brought me here. It is by His will I am in this strait place; in that I will rest." Next, "He will keep me here in His love, and give me grace in this trial to behave as His child." Then say, "He will make the trial a blessing, teaching me lessons He intends me to learn, and working in me the grace He means to bestow." And last, say, "In His good time He can bring me out again. How and when He knows."

Therefore say, "I am here by (1) God's appointment (2) in His keeping, (3) under His training and (4) for His time" (Michael Green, ed., *Illustrations for Biblical Preaching* [Grand Rapids, Mich.: Baker, 1989], 388).

If there is no situation that is desperate for God, there is, strictly speaking, no situation that is desperate for us. No matter how deep the water and high the mountains, God stands with us on the banks of the Red Sea.

I will sing unto the Lord, for He is highly exalted; The horse and its rider He has hurled into the sea. The Lord is my strength and song, and He has become my salvation; this is my God, and I will praise Him; my father's God, and I will extol Him. The Lord is a warrior; the Lord is His name.

EXODUS 15:1-3

SEVEN

When Our Bitter Waters Are Made Sweet

(Read Exodus 15)

The word *disappointment* is in everyone's vocabulary. We've all had dreams that have crashed around us. The bigger the dream, the bigger the disappointment.

Sometimes *people disappoint us.* Think of the woman who discovers that her husband is having an affair. She thought she knew him; she was convinced he would never cheat on her, but now her worst fears come to pass. She discovers that the one whom she loves has a secret life that was unknown to her. How deep is the betrayal! How difficult to rebuild trust!

Parents are often disappointed in children; an employer is disillusioned with the new manager he hired and the manager in turn is disappointed with his new boss.

Second, we are often *disappointed in circumstances.* When I joined the faculty of the Moody Bible Institute many years ago, the secretary for our section of faculty offices was a bright-eyed twenty-year-old woman whose cheerful smile greeted everyone who walked past her desk. Three months later a massive tumor was found in her abdomen. The doctors concluded that she had only three months to live.

She took the risk and accepted a new cancer treatment which seemed to work wonders. When she returned to work, all of us

105

rejoiced that her strength had returned. But the cancer reappeared and she died some months later.

Imagine being lifted to the heavens with rejuvenated strength only to be the more bitterly disappointed in the end. I often wondered why God allowed hope to grow so brightly just before it was so cruelly dashed to the ground. The promise of healing only increased the disappointment.

You expect a promotion and someone less qualified than you gets it; you anticipate making a deal and it falls through at the last moment. You never thought that your wife would have Alzheimer's disease. Disappointment.

Third, we may also be *disappointed in God*. A couple prayed for a child and were delighted when the young woman became pregnant. They fixed up the nursery complete with clothes and crib. But the baby died at birth. "God is no better than a plugged nickel to me," the man said angrily. "Why would He do this to us?"

Another woman who prayed for her children only to have her prayers unanswered said, "Long ago I gave up on God and I gave up on prayer. I don't even pray anymore, because I don't want to be disappointed."

The Israelites experienced severe disappointment (see Ex 15:22-27). Fresh from the miracle of the Red Sea, they sang a song of praise with such exuberance that we might think that they could believe in God for anything. But song turned to sighing; the music to murmuring. The heights of ecstasy only set them up for the depths of despair.

Tramping across the hot desert sand quickly reduced their supply of water. For three days they looked for an oasis but found none. Repeatedly the scouts came back with negative reports. Imagine the hot sand blinding their eyes and the wind blowing against them like a blast furnace. Anxiety was increasing.

Just when they had concluded that God was elusive and disinterested in their suffering, they spotted an oasis in the distance. Parents encouraged their children, "Just one more mile and we'll be there!" The younger ones ran the last few hundred yards so that they could be the first to drink. Some scooped up the water in their hands; others used containers.

Incredibly, though their tongues were parched with thirst, the water was so bitter they could not bring themselves to swallow it. Even today, we are told, there are oases where the water is so bitter that weary travelers cannot drink it. We read, "And when they came to Marah, they could not drink the waters of Marah, for they were bitter; therefore it was named Marah. So the people grumbled at Moses, saying, 'What shall we drink?'" (vv. 23-24).

Then the grumbling began. Why had Moses deceived them? Why was God playing games with them? Why had He led them to an oasis knowing that their hearts would soar in anticipation only to be cruelly disappointed? Better no oasis than one brimming with undrinkable, bitter waters.

What was God's purpose in this? We read, "There He made for them a statute and regulation, and there He tested them" (v. 25). This was a test, a college-level examination to reveal the degree of their commitment. It was to reveal what was in their hearts. Disappointment is exam time!

Disappointment reveals our character; it lets us know who we really are. It holds a mirror to our face so that we see ourselves, warts and all. Disappointment makes us either grow in faith or grumble in anger and unbelief.

Who led the Israelites to Marah? It was God, of course. They did not forge their own path through the desert. Every step was taken under the direction of Moses. And now, right in the center of God's will, just while they were following the map that God had spread out for them, they encountered this severe trial. God, they would learn, not only plans our successes but our disappointments too.

Of course, sometimes we are responsible for our own bitter disappointments. Even so, God stands ready to help us make the best of our own failures. As we've already learned, whether we are led to Marah by God or through our own foolish choices, our Lord stands ready to help us make the bitter waters sweet.

Someday we will stand before our own private Marah. We will expect to drink and find that we cannot. In exhaustion we will seek to be refreshed only to find hot desert sand blowing in our faces. The exuberance of the Red Sea is often followed by the bitter taste of Marah.

What do those experiences teach us? Why does God give disappointment such a high priority in His curriculum?

Disappointments Test Our Focus

When their hopes were dashed to the ground, the true hearts of the Israelites were revealed. In a pinch, they were not so much thinking about God as about their own needs. I'm not blaming them, because we would have been thinking about the water too. The problem was that their need for water was so all-consuming that they were not focusing on God, or at least they were not trusting Him. They jumped to the conclusion that He had abandoned them, rather than thinking that He just might have a refreshing surprise planned for them.

They erred in thinking that they did not have to trust God

when success was within their grasp. Whenever we have our hearts set on something, we stand a good chance of disappointment. You are convinced that you deserve that promotion; it's as good as done. Then it is given to someone who is less qualified than you. You are set to buy your dream house and it is sold from under your nose.

Or maybe your heart is set on marriage, but your intended partner leaves you. Or possibly a year after the wedding, you are disappointed in your mate. As the years pass, the differences grow and the relationship is further strained. Each month there is less hope that you will be fulfilled.

Whether it is the Israelites who were thirsty, or the single person who is lonely, or the workaholic who is married to his job, the temptation is always the same: It is to pin our hopes on something that will give us what we think we need. As a result, we live with the risk of deep disappointment. The more our hearts are consumed by what we want, the greater the possibility of a letdown.

Second, the hearts of the Israelites were not only set on water, but their hopes were also pinned on Moses. They were impressed with his leadership which had been marked by a number of different miracles; they thought that he would always come through for them. Now they felt deceived. Their adoration changed to grumbling. They blamed him even though the circumstances were not of his making.

If your happiness is dependent on another person—any person—you risk disillusionment. You might meet the woman whom you think you can't live without, only to find that she thinks she can do remarkably well without you. Or perhaps you marry the man of your dreams only to discover that your dream has turned into a nightmare.

On a list of ten reasons why marriages fail, unrealistic expectations is at the top. People expect a partner to do for them what only God can do, namely, to make them happy. You might think that these disappointments will never happen to you, but every human being is a potential broken reed.

The world has its superstars and so do we. We forget that Christ alone is our superstar; He alone is worthy of both our hopes and our affections. David, who had had his share of Marahs, wrote, "My soul, wait in silence for God only, for my hope is from Him" (Ps 62:5). Paul taught, "If then you have been raised up with Christ, keep seeking the things above, where Christ is, seated at the right hand of God. Set your mind on the things above, not on the things that are on earth" (Col 3:1-2). Even water should never mean more to us than God.

With their hopes pinned on Moses and their hearts fixed on slaking their thirst, the people knelt to drink; but when they choked, they became angry. Circumstances had not turned out as they were supposed to.

Disappointment is God's way of reminding us that there are idols in our lives we need to topple. Asaph was an Old Testament prophet who was envious of the wicked, but when he saw life from God's viewpoint he wrote, "Whom have I in heaven but Thee? And besides Thee, I desire nothing on earth. My flesh and my heart may fail, but God is the strength of my heart and my portion forever" (Ps 73:25-26).

Even the Marahs that we encounter in our pilgrimage are part of His plan. Thirst either drives us to God or makes us angry with Him. Nothing brings out the true state of our hearts more than being deprived of some basic need.

Disappointments Test Our Faith

What do you do with the bitterness? Moses was surrounded by hordes of angry people blaming him for their burning thirst. He shut them out and started talking to God.

> Then he cried out to the Lord, and the Lord showed him a tree; and he threw it into the waters, and the waters became sweet. There He made for them a statute and regulation, and there He tested them. And He said, "If you will give earnest heed to the voice of the Lord your God, and do what is right in His sight, and give ear to His commandments, and keep all His statutes, I will put none of the diseases on you which I have put on the Egyptians; for I, the Lord, am your healer."
>
> EXODUS 15:25-26

Whether the people believed God or not, Moses did. He showed his faith by crying to the Lord. When complained against, he didn't try to defend himself but referred the matter to His Master. Though hounded by an incited mob, he looked up.

Prayer is a mighty power that is swifter than an eagle, stronger than a lion. Prayer puts us in touch with the resources of a compassionate and holy God. And when Moses started praying, a miracle started happening.

God opened his eyes to a tree that he was to put into the water. It was just an ordinary tree made special by a divine command. With a splash, the bitter water was made sweet. The people drank to the full and were satisfied. This time, at least, their bitterness ended in blessing.

What relationship was there between this tree and the transformation of this oasis into fresh water? Some have speculated that it had a special bark that neutralized the acid in the water. But it is unlikely that there was any scientific link between the tree and the water. God did a miracle by making a connection that defied human reason. Throwing the tree into the water was a symbolic act, much like Moses holding his rod over the Red Sea. God changed the waters of Marah simply because He chose to do so.

God often changes our circumstances in response to prayer. The promotion you didn't receive turns out to be a blessing because a better opportunity comes your way. The rebellious child comes home, or a marriage is saved. In retrospect, it was a blessing that a girlfriend broke her relationship with you because God had someone better.

Sometimes God does an even greater miracle: *Rather than change our circumstances, He actually changes us so that we can accept our circumstances.* He enables us to forgive the drunkard who killed our child in a traffic accident. He enables us to accept a demotion without resentment. He gives us the ability to accept the sickness we are asked to endure. Sometimes He calms the sea and sometimes He lets the storm rage but calms our hearts. Our Marahs are designed to make us better, not bitter.

There is no water as sweet as that which once was bitter. There is nothing quite as satisfying as *hope* within despite the *heat* without. God remains sweet even when the water we are expected to drink is bitter. "In Thy presence is fulness of joy; in Thy right hand there are pleasures forever" (Ps 16:11).

Disappointments Test Our Faithfulness

God uses the occasion to give Israel the promise that if they will be obedient, they will be kept from the diseases that plague other nations: "I will put none of the diseases on you which I have put on the Egyptians; for I, the Lord, am your healer" (Ex 15:26).

In the law (particularly the Book of Leviticus), God gave specific regulations regarding such things as what the Israelites were to eat, how they were to dispense with waste, and how they were to wash themselves. God promised that if they followed these instructions, they would be healed, exempt from the diseases that plagued the Egyptians. This didn't mean that they would always be healed physically, since then they would not have had to die. God would, however, spare them from certain diseases during their days in the wilderness.

Some people today believe we can be healed from whatever sickness might plague us. They point to Isaiah 53:5, "by His scourging we are healed," as evidence that physical healing is our God-given right. However, elsewhere in the Bible it is clear that God does not always heal His people, and our complete redemption is yet in the future.

Eventually we will all be healed physically, when we receive our resurrected bodies. Until then, the frailty of the flesh is ever with us. For that matter, even our spiritual diseases will never be completely healed until we are transformed into glory, made complete in Christ. God heals our sinful hearts but even that process is never completed until we reach heaven. Where there is darkness, He shines light; where there is a wound, there is soothing oil. As the Great Physician of our souls He stands with us, enabling us to get as far in our spiritual journey as He wants us to go.

Your Marah and Mine

There are two important trees in the Bible. The first was the tree of the knowledge of good and evil, in the Garden of Eden. When Adam and Eve disobeyed God and ate of it, the whole stream of history became bitter. Sin contaminated everything from that time until now; we all have felt its poison in our soul.

The second tree is the cross. This tree is known for its blessing; it is the tree that reverses the curse that the tree of Eden caused. It is the only antidote to the poison that flows through the stream of history. It is a tree that absorbed the curse of sin and purified its waters.

Paul spoke of that tree: "Christ redeemed us from the curse of the Law, having become a curse for us, for it is written, 'Cursed is everyone who hangs on a tree'—in order that in Christ Jesus the blessing of Abraham might come to the Gentiles, so that we might receive the promise of the Spirit through faith" (Gal 3:13-14). Christ was cursed so that we could be blessed. The poison of sin was neutralized and healing was made available to all who believe.

Interestingly, when Jesus was on this tree He was offered wine mingled with myrrh (which in Hebrew is *marah*, bitter). This concoction was used as a sedative so that the pain of crucifixion might be alleviated. But Christ said no to it, because He wanted to die fully aware.

When Peter was trying to defend Christ that fateful evening on the Mount of Olives, Christ said, "Put the sword into the sheath; the cup which the Father has given Me, shall I not drink it?" (Jn 18:11). He said no to that cup offered on the cross so that He could drink the cup that the Father had given to Him. He drank that cup for us to its bitter dregs.

Death and the curse were in our cup
O Christ 'twas full for Thee
But thou hast drained the last dark drop
'Tis empty now for me.

What does the cross do? Like the tree used by Moses, it takes life with all of its bitterness and makes it sweet. It bears the precious fruit of the crucified Redeemer.

Sin is our most threatening disease. David made a parallel between sickness and sin: "Who pardons all your iniquities; who heals all your diseases" (Ps 103:3). The Prophet Isaiah when speaking of the nation Israel said, "From the sole of the foot even to the head there is nothing sound in it, only bruises, welts, and raw wounds, not pressed out or bandaged, nor softened with oil" (Is 1:6).

How does the cross make our bitter waters sweet? First, our sins are forgiven, and our troubled consciences are at rest. He speaks the word that we might be cleansed and made whole. Second, He heals the brokenhearted: "He heals the brokenhearted, and binds up their wounds. He counts the number of the stars; He gives names to all of them" (Ps 147:3-4).

The God who counts the stars heals our souls. The promises of God are the bandages God uses to heal the wounds of His people. There is healing for our sins and healing for the pain within our souls. All of this healing anticipates the future and final healing of redemption. In the end the bitter waters will be made sweet indeed.

The world has a variety of trees that are touted as cures, that will make the bitter waters sweet. High on the list is money: Win the lottery and no matter how terrible life is, you will live in uninterrupted bliss—that is, if you can get rid of your relatives! Yet, there was a couple in Canada who won $20 million and died six months later of cancer.

Another tree is pleasure: it grows, we are told, with deep and steady roots. It promises to remove the monotony of existence and replace it with excitement and glitter. Just nibble at it, people say, and you will find it much easier to make it from one weekend to another. But in the end this tree, though well-advertised, bears bitter fruit.

For years, drugs and alcohol were touted as the great escape from disappointment. But the increasing suicide rate is proof that these trees just add more poison to the bitter waters.

Many years ago an article in *Psychology Today* said, in effect, that it was healthy for some people to be out of touch with reality because reality was too depressing. If we can live comfortably in an illusionary world, it is a coping mechanism. In other words, for some people life is so bitter that they would best be served by pretending that it is sweet!

After Marah, the Israelites came to Elim, where there were twelve springs of water and seventy date palms (Ex 15:27). The thirsty Israelites discovered one spring for each of the tribes and enough date palms for everyone to enjoy a bite of fruit. On a map you can't see Elim from Marah, but God who knows the terrain had planned a special oasis up ahead.

A young Christian woman working in a church here in Chicago was brutally raped one summer evening. Years later she wrote her story, telling of how God had brought about healing; she is now happily married with several children. One of the questions she asked in retrospect was, *When I was so deeply wounded, why did someone not tell me that some day the sun would shine again? Why didn't someone tell me that someday I would be emotionally whole?* Her question, in effect, was, *When*

I was at Marah, why didn't someone tell me that I would eventually get to Elim?

Next to your Marah, there is a tree that can make the bitter waters sweet. Your *disappointment* might well be God's *appointment* to prove that blessing can follow bitterness.

The closer we are to God the more quickly we can march from Marah to Elim. The God who leads us into the desert also leads us to a refreshing oasis.

EIGHT

Living With an Attitude of Gratitude

(Read Exodus 16)

Nothing is easier than faultfinding, it takes no talent, no self-denial; no brains and no character are required to get set up in the grumbling business," said Robert West.

Six weeks into the desert, the Israelites had to bid farewell to Elim with its seventy palm trees and twelve water springs. As they made their trek through the wilderness, they discovered they could not live off their memories, wonderful as those memories were. When their food supply dwindled, they felt stranded and betrayed. No matter how many miracles God had done for them, they did not have the confidence that He would provide for their future. Hunger and hot sand made their faith evaporate. Complaining is contagious.

And the whole congregation of the sons of Israel grumbled against Moses and Aaron in the wilderness. And the sons of Israel said to them "Would that we had died by the Lord's hand in the land of Egypt, when we sat by the pots of meat, when we ate bread to the full; for you have brought us out into this wilderness to kill this whole assembly with hunger."

EXODUS 16:2-3

A few tongues began to wag and soon everyone was caught up with this national uproar. Like poison sprinkled into a water supply, the murmuring spread.

Their complaint was directed toward God's appointed leader, Moses. They cynically accused him of bringing them into the desert to watch them die. To have died in Egypt, they said, would have been better than dying of hunger in the blistering sun.

Moses felt the sharp sting of their complaint. They intended to hurt him and they did. No matter that he had risked his life for them; no past sacrifice could erase their present anger. The miracles of yesterday were apparently of no help in seeing a miracle today. God had met their need for water at Marah, but they evidently did not believe He could take care of their need for bread.

God gave the people a surprising reply. "I have heard the grumblings of the sons of Israel; speak to them, saying, 'At twilight you shall eat meat, and in the morning you shall be filled with bread; and you shall know that I am the Lord your God'" (v. 12).

First, He assured them that He would feed them; in fact, bread would be rained on them from heaven. In the morning there would be manna, and meat would be given in the evening. Their complaint had been duly registered and God would respond.

But second, and most important, God was upset with their attitude. Though they directed their complaint to Moses, they were actually being critical of the Almighty. Moses said, "For the Lord hears your grumbling which you grumble against Him. And what are we? Your grumblings are not against us but against the Lord" (v. 8). Logically, it must be so, for Moses was

God's representative. Therefore, to complain against Moses was to complain against God.

Just think: It was the pillar of cloud that led them into the barren wilderness where there was neither water nor food. Moses, who followed God's instructions, could hardly be blamed for taking a sharp turn into the wilderness. God had promised to take them all the way to Canaan and this was the route He chose. They were hungry by divine appointment.

Though we usually don't think of it this way, complaining against circumstances is complaining against God. Even when men curse the weather, they are unwittingly cursing God. Who, after all, is in charge of the wind, the hail, or the sunshine? Even when we grumble about our health, our difficulties at work, or our lack of money, we are implicating God since He has all of these circumstances under His supervision and control. Even the very hairs of our head are numbered.

Certainly there are some things we can change, but they are few in number in comparison with the many things that are well beyond our reach and control. God had led the Israelites to the edge of despair that they might get closer to Him. He knew that *we usually do not trust Him unless we have to.* Blessed are those who are convinced that everything is under His sovereign control.

In this case God made sure that the Israelites would have to trust Him every single day. They would be given just enough bread for each day so they could never become complacent. "Behold I will rain bread from heaven for you; and the people shall go out and gather a day's portion every day, that I may test them, whether or not they will walk in My instruction" (v. 4). Not until they were in a tight corner did God open the door. And they would be in a tight corner every day.

God chose to feed the Israelites because of His promise to bring them into the land. I know of no other period in history where God fed His people with manna from heaven. In our day God's people have often starved to death or have been put to death by evil men. God promises only that He will walk with us through the fire, not that we shall be exempt from it.

In Exodus 15 God let the Israelites be thirsty; in this chapter he let them be hungry. God chose to test them with the very essentials of life. He taught them that their very existence was daily held in His caring hands. If we want to delight God's heart, we must trust Him; we must believe that He will be there for us no matter what.

How was this experience designed to get the nation of Israel closer to God?

They Were to Trust His Leading

We've already learned that since God was their map and compass, they were in the desert by divine appointment. The cloud guided them by day and the pillar of fire by night. God would not lead them to a place where He could not keep them. He would not abandon His adopted children. His integrity was at stake.

God tested the Israelites, but of course this was a mighty test for Moses too. Think of the responsibility that weighed on his shoulders. During his days in Midian, Moses experienced the barrenness of the desert and knew that not so much as a single family could survive apart from a series of miracles. To believe God for himself was one thing; to believe God for the whole congregation was quite another.

Apparently, Moses believed but the Israelites did not. They nostalgically longed for Egypt and compared it with their present predicament. They forgot the beatings; they did not remember how they had hunted for straw like scavengers to make the full quota of bricks. They forgot their humiliation, their powerlessness, and their pain. All they could think of were the pots of meat. For now, at least, Egypt looked better than the wilderness. "Would that we had died by the Lord's hand in the land of Egypt!" they intoned (v. 3).

They also forgot the song of triumph they had sung after crossing the Red Sea. They forgot how the water was sweetened at Marah, and the wonderful provision at Elim. They blocked their miraculous past out of their minds and could see only the sand that lay before them. Their memories were no better than their eyes.

Satan wants us to distort the past, to remember the cheap thrills of our Egypt experience. He wants us to forget that we were "deceived, enslaved to various lusts and pleasures, spending our life in malice and envy, hateful, hating one another" (Ti 3:3). To blot out the memory of the bitter taste of sin is one of the devil's oldest strategies. We forget that *it is better to be in a barren desert by the will of God than to be fed at the smorgasbord offered by Satan and the world.*

The congregation distorted the past and feared the future. They expected to die of starvation in the wilderness. They felt deceived and angry with their leaders and angry with their God. With their memories riveted on yesterday and their emotions in flux about tomorrow, the possibilities of the present moment evaporated like steam from a boiling kettle.

Someone has said that many people live their lives crucified between two thieves: the regrets of yesterday and the anxieties of tomorrow. If we are focused on either the past or the future, we cannot enjoy the present. Our past almost always stands to condemn us; our future is always uncertain. And if we believe the worst about tomorrow (as all of us are prone to do), we will face only darkness. A pessimist, it is said, can hardly wait for the future so that he can look back on it with regret!

The Lord was testing the Israelites, saying in effect, "You have seen My glory in leading you out of Egypt with signs and wonders, why cannot you believe Me for your future? With one hand I will lead you into the desert that you might be hungry; with the other hand I will feed you."

Moses was learning that God was not merely the One who could deliver His people, He was the One who could sustain them as well. The map from Egypt to Canaan did not only include the Red Sea but the desert. They would have strength as long as the journey would last.

If only they had remembered that they were in a tight place by divine appointment. And as I have emphasized in a previous chapter, God is just as ready to help us in a tight place that is of our own making as He is to help us in those tight places into which He has led us.

Even hunger can be a divine appointment.

They Were to Trust His Feeding

God had promised Abraham, Isaac, and Jacob that He would bring their descendants into the land that would be their possession forever. Was there any chance that He would not provide? Of course not. The invisible hand of divine providence was always working to make sure that the nation would survive. The responsibility of finding bread fell on God.

We've learned that in response to their complaining, God promised them bread and meat. The next morning, after the sun evaporated the dew, small round cakes dotted the ground. The people didn't know what it was and asked, "What is it?" (in Hebrew, *man hu*) Moses explained that this was the bread God had given to them. It looked like a coriander seed and tasted like wafers made with honey. Because it was sent from heaven, the psalmist Asaph referred to it as "the bread of angels" (Ps 78:25).

Two instructions were given concerning the manna. First, each person was to gather just enough for himself and his family. "And the sons of Israel did so, and some gathered much and some little. When they measured it with an omer, he who had gathered much had no excess and he who had gathered little had no lack" (Ex 16:17-18). The rabbis interpreted this to mean that whatever quantity a man might gather, when he measured it in his tent, he had just as much as he needed to give an omer (about two quarts) to every person in the house. Centuries later, Christ miraculously fed a multitude and yet asked that the fragments be gathered that nothing be lost.

Second, they were not to store any of the manna for the next day; if they did, it would breed worms and become foul. The one exception was on the sixth day when they were permitted to gather enough for two days (the next day was the Sabbath when no work was to be done). So the manna remained extra fresh on that day by the meticulous hand of God. This provision gives incidental evidence that the Sabbath was actually kept even before the giving of the Law on Sinai.

What could be clearer than these instructions? Yet some of the people simply did not believe God's word, but had to test

His instructions for themselves. Some tried to hoard the manna until the next day and discovered that it did breed worms! And they also went out on the Sabbath to gather manna only to discover that there was none on the ground. They had to learn by experience that God knew what He was talking about.

These miracles continued day after day, week after week, and year by year for the duration of the wilderness journey. Only when they arrived in Canaan did the supply of manna end because the land itself was able to sustain them. For now they had to learn that God takes care of His people even when they are consigned to a barren land.

In the evening God supplied meat by sending quail that flew so close to the ground that they could be caught. These small birds resemble partridges and even today migrate from southern Israel and Arabia to central Africa. Egyptian art depicts people catching the birds in hand-held nets.

Despite all of this, there were times when the complaining of the congregation continued. In an incident that probably happened later, God became very angry because of their demands. Again, the topic was food; this time it was a desire for meat. As their complaints became louder, Moses became more despondent. He passed their complaints on to the Almighty:

> So Moses said to the Lord, "Why hast Thou been so hard on Thy servant? And why have I not found favor in Thy sight, that Thou hast laid the burden of all this people on me? Was it I who conceived all this people? Was it I who brought them forth, that Thou shouldest say to me, 'Carry them in your bosom as a nurse carries a nursing infant,' to the land which Thou didst swear to their fathers? Where am I to get meat to give to all this people? For they weep before

me, saying, 'Give us meat that we may eat!' I alone am not able to carry all this people, because it is too burdensome for me. So if Thou art going to deal thus with me, please kill me at once, if I have found favor in Thy sight, and do not let me see my wretchedness."

NUMBERS 11:11-15

God gave Moses two replies. First, seventy elders would assist Moses in giving leadership in the desert. Moses had been carrying the burdens of the people all alone (Aaron's help was minimal). Moses was trying to resolve all of the disputes, listening to all the complaints, and representing the needs of the people to God. Little wonder he was exhausted.

The second part of the answer was given in anger: Yes, the people would be given meat to eat. In fact, the Lord said, "You shall eat, not one day, nor two days, nor five days, nor ten days, nor twenty days, but a whole month, until it comes out of your nostrils and becomes loathsome to you; because you have rejected the Lord who is among you and have wept before Him, saying, 'Why did we ever leave Egypt?'" (Ex 16:19-20). Then a wind came and brought quail from the sea and the birds flew within three feet of the ground and were caught by the Israelites.

So far so good. The people were hungry for meat and God gave them their heart's desire. But after hoarding more than they could possibly eat and then gorging themselves we read, "While the meat was still between their teeth, before it was chewed, the anger of the Lord was kindled against the people, and the Lord struck the people with a very severe plague. So the name of that place was called Kibrothhattaavah, because there they buried the people who had been greedy" (vv. 33-34).

The sin of the people was not that they wanted meat, but that they wanted it more than they wanted the will of God. True, they were hungry, but they should not have complained against God, nor should they have been so greedy once the quail were sent to them. The psalmist comments, "They quickly forgot His works; they did not wait for His counsel, but craved intensely in the wilderness, and tempted God in the desert. So He gave them their request, but sent a wasting disease among them" (Ps 106:13-15). When we are selfish in our praying, God just might answer our request and give us grief besides!

There is something even more important than having our desires granted; namely, submitting those desires to a God who knows better than we do. As the saying goes, He gives what is best to those who leave the choice with Him.

Neither the manna nor the meat could be hoarded. If kept beyond a day, it bred worms. God did not want them to live so much as a single day without dependence on Him. They needed to be kept from the sin of independence, the pride that would make them forget God. By nature we would prefer to have enough stored up so that we would not have to pray, "Give us this day our daily bread."

The more we hoard, the more likely we are to drift away from God rather than be nudged in His direction. Without daily spiritual provision, our life will soon become stale and breed worms.

I am greatly blessed when I worship with believers on Sunday; but I've also learned that manna cannot easily be carried over to Monday morning. Regardless of how much spiritual food I may digest on Sunday, I have sometimes failed spiritually on Monday because I did not enjoy fresh fellowship with God.

Later a pot of manna was put in the ark as a reminder of

God's faithfulness. Generations to come could meditate on the lessons learned by a fledgling nation that needed God so desperately in the wilderness.

God Wanted Them to Trust His Pruning

What was God's hidden agenda in the wilderness? Why did He not supply water even before they became thirsty? Why did He not supply manna before they became hungry? Why did He bring them to the edge of despair before He rescued them?

As always, God's arrow was aimed at their hearts. He wanted to draw the nation closer to Him; He knew that if they didn't have to wait for their blessings, they would soon forget their source. Here is the divine interpretation:

> And you shall remember all the way which the Lord your God has led you in the wilderness these forty years, that He might humble you, testing you, to know what was in your heart, whether you would keep His commandments or not. And He humbled you and let you be hungry, and fed you with manna which you did not know, nor did your fathers know, that He might make you understand that man does not live by bread alone, but man lives by everything that proceeds out of the mouth of the Lord. Your clothing did not wear out on you, nor did your foot swell these forty years. Thus you are to know in your heart that the Lord your God was disciplining you just as a man disciplines his son. Therefore, you shall keep the commandments of the Lord your God, to walk in His ways and to fear Him.
>
> DEUTERONOMY 8:2-6

When I say that God wanted them to trust His pruning, I mean that God was making them into a nation that would bear spiritual fruit. He had planted the seed of faith in their hearts and He wanted to nurture it. Since both sunshine and rain are needed for a garden, God created the optimum conditions for growth. The experiences of the desert were part of the cultivation, watering, and cutting off of the dead branches.

Or we could put it this way: Gardeners know that weeds must be pulled if plants are to grow and eventually bear fruit. The heat and hunger of the desert revealed the weeds that would stifle growth. God already knew what was in their hearts, but these trials would be used like a mirror so that the people would see themselves for what they were. Some would be smitten with conviction and repent; others would persist in their stubbornness and be judged.

Just as iron ore is heated to separate the gold from the dross, so God wanted to purify His people. God wanted to turn up the heat so that the scum might come to the surface. Heat and hunger bring out the best and worst in all of us.

We don't know whether these trials achieved their intended result. We are left with the impression that most of the Israelites continued their complaining without developing the faith that is so precious to God. On the other hand, there may have been many who looked to God and did not join in the complaining and unbelief. These trials separated the faithful and the faithless.

Moses, Joshua, and Caleb were clear examples of those who believed they would yet see the glorious provision of God. They were at odds with hundreds of thousands of others who were disgruntled, complaining whenever they did not see the bread in their hands or the water in their buckets. As always, there was an invisible line that divided the faithful from the unfaithful, those who drew near from those who turned away.

Our Example

How should the Israelites have responded to the blight around them? Where can we turn for an example of how to handle the heat and hunger of the wilderness?

Christ was in the wilderness for only forty days in contrast to the forty years experienced by the Israelites. But He experienced an intensity of hunger that the ancient people could never have imagined. "Then Jesus was led up by the Spirit into the wilderness to be tempted by the devil. And after He had fasted forty days and forty nights, He then became hungry" (Mt 4:1-2). Not a word of complaint passed from His lips.

Understandably, the devil tried to exploit Christ's hunger, taunting Him, "If You are the Son of God, command that these stones become bread" (v. 3). Christ might have appealed to His rights. As the second member of the Trinity, He had a right to have every one of His desires fulfilled. He had the right to do miracles.

But Christ saw the temptation for what it was: An attempt to have a legitimate need met in an illegitimate way. Satan longed to see Christ have a desire fulfilled without submitting that request to the divine will. Christ quoted directly from the same passage in Deuteronomy that gave the reason for Israel's hunger and thirst. "Man shall not live on bread alone, but on every word that proceeds out of the mouth of God" (v. 4, cf. Dt 8:3).

There are some things in life that are even more important

than eating; indeed, *it is better to starve within the will of God than eat and be satisfied apart from it.* Disobedience is a greater curse than hunger. Christ knew that His life was in the hands of His Father, and that was enough to nourish Him.

From where can we derive this strength to make the right choices, to submit our physical desires to the will of God? We must cultivate a spiritual appetite. There is a hidden manna that makes the manna of the desert seem tasteless. And as we eat of it, our taste buds will develop.

To the Pharisees and anyone else who cared to listen, Christ said,

> Truly, truly, I say to you, it is not Moses who has given you the bread out of heaven, but it is My Father who gives you the true bread out of heaven. For the bread of God is that which comes down out of heaven, and gives life to the world.... I am the bread of life; he who comes to Me shall not hunger, and he who believes in Me shall never thirst.
>
> JOHN 6:32-33,35

We can submit our physical desires to God because He gives us strength in the inner man. There is a bread that others cannot understand, a bread more precious than the food we so naturally crave.

Like Israel, we cannot eat once and be satisfied; we cannot slake our thirst on Sunday and expect it will do for the rest of the week. Just as we must eat regularly to sustain our outer man, so we must eat to keep the inner man in good health.

Let every one of us begin our day by feeding on the heavenly manna through meditation on the Word of Christ. Once we lose those moments, the rest of our day will crash upon us and our consciousness of Christ will be disrupted. As F.B. Meyer says, "Each man needs all that a new day can yield him of God's grace and comfort. It must be daily bread."

We must recapture the habit of beginning each day with the manna needed to sustain us. Someone has written:

> I met God in the morning when the day was at its best
>> And His presence came like sunrise, like a glory in my breast.
>> All day long His presence lingered, all day long He stayed with me
>> I sailed in perfect calmness o'er a troubled sea.
>> Other ships were blown and battered, other ships were sore distressed
>> But the winds that seemed to drive them, brought to me a perfect rest.
>> Then I thought of other mornings, with a keen remorse of mind
>> When I too had loosed the moorings with His presence left behind.
>> So I think I know the secret learned from many a troubled way
>> You must seek Him in the morning if you want Him through the day.

Those who are serious about getting closer to God know that yesterday's nourishment will not do for today. The Almighty draws us to Himself so that we might be fed again.

NINE

Using Our Weapons to Win

(Read Exodus 17:8-16)

I n war, there is no substitute for victory," said General Douglas MacArthur when he addressed the United States Congress on April 19, 1951. To weaken the enemy is not enough; a battle must be fought with the intention of winning, even at high cost.

Every one of us is fighting some battle. We may be in the throes of a broken relationship. Or there may be conflict within our family, among our relatives. Just today I spoke with a woman who is in a bitter custody battle with her ex-husband, whom she believes has abused the children. She is going to court to gain permanent custody, but she has no assurance as to how the judge will rule. Her battle will be long and will drain her emotionally. No telling what it will do to her children.

Perhaps your battle is with circumstances, ill health, or financial setbacks. Perhaps it is a conflict at work, or a secret struggle within the soul. Sometimes those inner battles appear small, but they might begin a series of temptations that will lead to losing a bigger battle in the future. No one commits an armed robbery who did not begin with petty thievery. No one commits murder without having nurtured hatred within the heart. No one commits immorality without violating a series of boundaries that eventually led to the act. Yes, the little sins, if left unjudged, lead inevitably to the larger ones.

How Do We Fight? And, How Do We Fight to Win?

The Israelites had a series of enemies that correspond to our enemies today. Egypt represents the world. It was a monotonous country with sand and little relief from the hot sun. Worse, it was a country of slavery where the people worked without enjoying the benefits of their labors. There was futility, helplessness, and despair. It was a land of broken promises.

Pharaoh controlled the lives of the Israelites in Egypt. The king, as we have learned, was worshiped though he was an enemy of the true God. He offered the people compromises, only to give himself time to regroup and tighten his hold on their lives. Like Satan, Pharaoh wanted to give an inch so that he could gain a foot.

In the years ahead, the Israelites would encounter another enemy, namely, the Canaanites. Canaan does not represent heaven; when we arrive in glory, we will not have to conquer any Jerichos. Canaan represents the life of a believer in Christ, conquering territory in the name of the Lord. We have to fight our Canaanites too, if we wish to enjoy our inheritance.

But for now, there was another enemy that was slowly demoralizing the Israelites and had the potential of destroying them. The Amalekites were standing in the way of Israel's journey to the Land of Promise. At Rephidim the Israelites fought their first battle since leaving Egypt. Here was another test they would have to pass to see God's promise fulfilled.

Just before this battle, the Israelites had another scare in the desert when their water supply ran out. Just as at Marah, the people quarreled with Moses, asking him once more why he had brought them into the desert to see them die of thirst. This time Moses was told to strike a rock with his rod and water flowed. (This incident along with a similar experience will be considered in chapter 13 of this book.)

While basking in the joy of a miracle, the Israelites were now confronted by a warring tribe intent on a smashing victory. We read, "Then Amalek came and fought against Israel at Rephidim" (Ex 17:8). Even though there may have been enough territory for both tribes in this fertile oasis, the Amalekites saw Israel as a threat that needed to be eliminated. The Israelites felt intimidated and quite helpless.

This conflict has some essential lessons for our own private battles. We won't start winning those battles until we learn the lessons Moses has to teach us.

Know Your Enemy

Who were the Amalekites? They were descendants of Esau, the man of this world who sold his birthright for a bowl of lentil soup. You will remember that Esau and Jacob were twins who were destined for conflict. Before their birth, a prophecy was given to their mother Rebecca that "the older shall serve the younger" (Gn 25:23). Years later Esau, who was a hunter, came in from the field and was so famished that he agreed to give his birthright to his brother for just a bowl of stew!

What was the birthright Esau despised? The promise that through Abraham and his descendants all the families of the earth would be blessed. This covenant would culminate in the birth of Christ through the line of David. Perhaps Esau thought that this promise was not only impractical but too far distant. No matter what God had said, it did not help him at this moment when his famished body needed food. He was a practical man, a man of action, a man who wanted what he wanted—*now.* The present was more important than an unseen future. He thought he had all that it took to be a man apart from God; living for the moment was stern business. Esau lived by his own rules and died by them.

Like William Henley said in his poem, "Invictus":

It matters not how straight the gate,
How charged with punishment the scroll;
I am the master of my fate,
I am the captain of my soul.

Impulse and gratification drove Esau to make an agreement with his brother. In exchange for the soup that was in the pot, Jacob could have the blessings of inheritance. Esau's rebellious attitude was passed on to his descendants. He had a son named Eliphaz whose concubine Timna bore him a son named Amalek (36:12).

And so it was that the Amalekites did not fear God, but sought to exterminate the Israelites. They represent all who would elevate the flesh above the spirit; they are symbolic of any one of us who would jeopardize our relationship with God in exchange for an immediate and selfish impulse. Though the Amalekites were finally exterminated during the days of Hezekiah, the spirit of Amalek lives on.

Back to the story: This warring tribe now sought to bar the Israelites from marching toward the Promised Land. So we read,

So Moses said to Joshua, "Choose men for us, and go out, fight against Amalek. Tomorrow I will station myself on the top of the hill with the staff of God in my hand." And Joshua did as Moses told him, and fought against Amalek; and Moses, Aaron, and Hur went up to the top of the hill. So it came about when Moses held his hand up, that Israel prevailed, and when he let his hand down, Amalek prevailed.

EXODUS 17:9-11

Just as the flesh resists every effort of the Holy Spirit to lead us into a more intimate walk with God, so Amalek was intent on blocking the path of the Israelites.

What strategy did Amalek use? Many years later, Moses gave an inspired commentary on this battle. "Remember what Amalek did to you along the way when you came out of Egypt, how he met you along the way and attacked among you all the stragglers at your rear when you were faint and weary; and he did not fear God" (Dt 25:17-18).

Amalek attacked *suddenly*. There was no warning, no hint as to when the soldiers would strike. Vicious warriors hung around near the back side of the Israelites, doing as much damage as they could while trying to avoid personal injury. The Israelites would wake up in the morning and discover that some of their people had been killed during the night. No one knew when the next attack would come.

Satan uses the same strategy against us. Seldom does anyone wake up in the morning and say, "Today I intend to disobey God." No, the temptation tends to sneak up on us. A man who committed adultery about a month ago said, "I never planned that this would ever happen to me." But happen it has.

Spiritually speaking, we must be ready for the surprise attack. At one moment we might be worshiping God and moments later the temptations might be overwhelming. Peter, who had experienced his own share of failures, wrote, "Be of sober spirit, be on the alert. Your adversary, the devil, prowls about like a roaring lion, seeking someone to devour. But resist him, firm in your faith, knowing that the same experiences of suffering are being accomplished by your brethren who are in the world (1 Pt 5:8-9). Watch for the unexpected attack!

Second, the Amalekites attacked *defiantly*. Following some impressive triumphs, the warriors were emboldened to attack Israel "right in their face." This was not just a physical battle, a skirmish over territory. We read that Amalek "did not fear God" (Dt 25:18). More specifically, we know that they were followers of another god, Satan, who has always tried to do all that he could to destroy God's people.

Battles often follow blessings. The Israelites had just been given the gift of manna and the rock had just brought forth water. We might think that this would have been a time when they were spiritually strong, but they were vulnerable. After all, when everything is going well, our personal satisfaction often distracts us from complete dependence on God. The word *Rephidim* means "resting place." When the Israelites thought they could rest, they drew enemy fire. In fact, Moses remembered that this battle took place when Israel was "faint and weary" (Ex 17:18).

Blessings bring dangers. Abraham was blessed in Canaan, but when a famine came he went to Egypt in disobedience to God. Elijah saw God win an impressive victory over the prophets of Baal, and yet days later he ran away, fearing the anger of Jezebel. Satan drove Christ into the desert immediately after He heard the blessed words of His Father, "This is My Son in whom I am well pleased." Sometimes I think Satan says to himself, "I want to find a Christian whom God has particularly blessed, so that I can attack!"

If you are enjoying uninterrupted blessings without any conflict, then it may be that, (a) Satan does not think you are important to God's cause in the world; or, (b) he may be setting you up for an attack tomorrow. All sunshine makes a desert. The storms must come to disturb our cloudless skies.

Tomorrow may be your day. Thoughts may come to mind that may even be a surprise to you. You may be tempted to do things that you have always condemned others for; you may be tempted to do what you just knew you could never do. Plans for your downfall are already being laid.

Third, Amalek attacked *strategically*. The enemy did not make random forays into the Israelite camp. He did not attack on the front lines where the strongest soldiers were. He aimed for the weakest members of the Israelite band.

God tests us in our strengths to make us even stronger; Satan tempts us in our weaker parts to bring us down. He will push the door that is most easily opened. Every time we succumb to a temptation, the propensity to do it again will become stronger. Sin, someone has said, takes us farther than we wanted to go, keeps us longer than we intended to stay, and costs us more than we intended to pay.

What is your weak point? What is the one sin you find the hardest to resist? Expect a devastating attack right there. Jesus said, "Watch and pray that ye enter not into temptation."

The more Moses knew about Amalek the better. Strategy must be tailored to the enemy. And yet, as we shall see, behind the battle in the valley there was a simultaneous battle on the hilltop. We need more than one weapon if we intend to win. One set of weapons works for the valley, but another has to be used above the fray.

Use Your Weapons

Visualize a city that is continually under attack from the enemy. About every other week, soldiers climb through a hole in the southeast wall and wreak havoc among the inhabitants. Don't you think that the city council would have enough sense to strengthen that part of the wall? Yet countless Christians are defeated by the same sin week after week and never think about a strategy for winning.

Let's take a page from the life of Moses. Now at the age of eighty-one, he told Joshua to fight Amalek in the valley while he went to intercede on the hilltop. With the staff of God in his hand (that ordinary staff that had now been made famous), he walked to the top of the hill. He was not shirking his duty. He knew what Joshua needed to do, but he also knew what *he* needed to do. We read,

> So it came about when Moses held his hand up, that Israel prevailed, and when he let his hand down, Amalek prevailed. But Moses' hands were heavy. Then they took a stone and put it under him, and he sat on it; and Aaron and Hur supported his hands, one on one side and one on the other. Thus his hands were steady until the sun set. So Joshua overwhelmed Amalek and his people with the edge of the sword.
>
> EXODUS 17:11-13

What an example of the weapons needed in a war!

First, we learn that we need the sword in the valley. For Joshua and the Israelites it was a sharpened stone used against the enemy in hand-to-hand combat. This is the first time Joshua is mentioned in the Bible. He had been born in Egypt, and was now forty-five years old. Moses felt comfortable in turning to him when the situation called for bravery and leadership. Here he is a soldier; at Kadesh Barnea he will become a spy; later he will be a successor to Moses. He did exactly as Moses had told him, for he "wholly followed the Lord."

This conflict in the valley could not have been avoided. The Israelites could not have walked away hoping that the enemy would respond in kind. Let's remember that the enemies of God are not only interested in self-preservation but have a compulsive desire to see the living God dethroned. There had to be a battle, a fight to the finish.

I've known Christians who think that if they leave the devil alone, he will leave them alone. What these believers don't realize is that Satan does not leave any of God's children alone. Every Christian is involved in the battle; to think otherwise is a confession of surrender. We're all involved directly in combat. Like Amalek, Satan stalks us, hoping to strike a mortal blow.

We don't use a sharpened stone, but we do use the Sword of the Spirit which is the Word of God. As Paul put it, "For our struggle is not against flesh and blood, but against the rulers, against the powers, against the world forces of this darkness, against the spiritual forces of wickedness in the heavenly places" (Eph 6:12). Then he goes on to describe six pieces of armor we need if we intend to stand in the victory Christ has won for us. Among them, of course is "the Sword of the Spirit, which is the Word of God" (v. 17). If we could talk with Moses, he would tell us that we can't fight without a sword. Joshua needed his, we need ours.

Second, we also need the staff of God on the hilltop. When Moses raised his hands, Joshua prevailed; when he put down his hand, the enemy prevailed. What was the relationship between the physical battle in the valley and the spiritual battle on the hilltop?

Some think that the lifting up of the hands was a signal for advancement; to drop his hands was a signal for surrender. Others have suggested that the lifting up of the hands was also the sign of an oath; to drop the hands would have been a sign of retreat.

But the most common meaning is that of the lifting up of hands in prayer. "So I will bless Thee as long as I live; I will lift up my hands in Thy name" (Ps 63:4). Paul told Timothy that churches should pray, "Therefore I want the men in every place to pray, lifting up holy hands, without wrath and dissension" (1 Tm 2:8). Moses was reaching out to God in intercession. Only prayer can account for the invisible connection between the valley and the hilltop.

If a television camera had been there to capture a newsreel of the battle, the observers would have noticed how the strategic advantage alternated between the Israelites and the Amalekites. And then to the surprise of everyone (a perceptive person might have noticed) an old man could be seen on a distant hilltop. Whenever he raised his hands, Israel would advance; whenever he lowered them, the Amalekites would strike back with terrifying force. The discussion that evening would have been: What possible relationship could there be between the raised hand of one man and the defeat or victory of two million people? Military strategists would have been confounded.

Moses knew the power of prayer, but he became weary. So Aaron and Hur set Moses on a rock which made him low enough for them to be able to keep his hands raised. In all, three men were changing the direction of the battle.

How desperately we need Aarons and Hurs to hold up the

leadership of local churches and the cause of Christ at large! Just think: The prayers (or lack of them) of one person can affect the spiritual outcome of a great congregation. There is a hidden connection between prayer and the victories we celebrate.

Some have seen in this story a picture of Christ, who ascended into heaven and represents us before the Father. Of course Christ never becomes weary, but we do. While on earth, Jesus invited Peter, James, and John to intercede with Him in Gethsemane, but they kept falling asleep. We read, "And He came to the disciples and found them sleeping, and said to Peter, 'So, you men could not keep watch with Me for one hour? Keep watching and praying, that you may not enter into temptation; the spirit is willing, but the flesh is weak'" (Mt 26:40-41).

Moses would agree. The flesh resists the spirit, particularly when we kneel to pray.

Let's not overlook the balance between the valley and the hilltop. Do we fight against Satan or do we just "rest in the Lord" through prayer? The answer is that we fight in prayer, but we also fight in our work for Christ. We not only pray about circumstances but we actually seek to change them. As has been said, we pray as if it all depends on God, but then we work as though it all depends on us.

The mystic would have told the soldiers to abandon the valley. He would have insisted that prayer alone was all that was needed. God could sovereignly win the victory whether soldiers were conscripted to fight or not. The battle, the mystic would say, is wholly the Lord's.

The man who thinks that "God helps those who help themselves" would have stressed that only what happened in the valley really mattered. He would have argued, quite plausibly, that there is no scientific connection between an old man with his hands raised on a hilltop and victory or defeat in the valley. He would have rallied the troops and told them the battle was wholly in their hands.

God, of course, makes a direct connection between the prayers of His people and their victories and defeats. You and I can't win in the valley unless we also win on the hilltop. Weariness in prayer means weakness in battle.

Our intercession is not like a cellular phone with a limited radius. Through prayer, we can travel across the ocean and stand beside a missionary; we can enter into a high-rise and pray for a child who is being abused; we can touch the life of a relative whose address we have lost. Prayer that moves the hand of God moves the world.

A couple who had given up a child for adoption described the agony of knowing they gave birth to a child whom they will never see. A child who, quite possibly, will not come to know Christ as Savior. What they wouldn't give to hold that child in their arms for one hour! But I assured them that they could still have a profound influence in that child's life. God knew his whereabouts and through prayer they could touch his life. God sees the battle in the valley just as clearly as the prayers offered on the hilltop.

Martin Luther prayed, "Dear Lord, although I am sure of my position, I am unable to sustain it without Thee. Help me or I am lost." Yes, God knows who we are; He knows our weaknesses and our strengths. He knows we can win against our Amalek.

The valleys of today are filled with every spiritual and moral battle imaginable. When we lose, we pour more resources into the valley; we raise our voices, we angrily shout for our rights.

Churches have been known to depend on the same need-driven strategies as the business world. Many volunteer for the valley but few volunteer for the hilltop. We have many organizers but few "agonizers."

Our God-given weapons are to be used so that our Amalek will not rob us of the Promised Land. Winning means we know our weapons and use them.

Follow Your Leader

When the war was won, Moses built an altar and named it "The Lord Is My Banner" (Ex 17:15). He not only wanted God to receive the credit but he knew that the nation needed a point of identification; the altar was a visual reminder of the need to march under the direction of the sovereign Lord.

High up in the mountains of Liechtenstein (a small sliver of land between Germany and Switzerland), there is a castle with special limited access. We are told that when the flag is flying, the king is in residence; when he is absent, the flag is taken down. The flag is a sign of the presence of the king.

When my wife and I visited Liechtenstein, the flag was visible on the pole but the wind was so calm that it hung limp next to the pole. Only when the wind was blowing would we see its colors.

So today, many people claim to march under God's flag, but their commitment is largely a secret. Only when the wind begins to blow can we see who the true followers of Christ are. When we march under Christ's banner, we affirm His presence. Committed citizens salute when the flag is raised.

When the Lord places His banner over us, everyone we meet

should know to whom we belong. The primary difference between Israel and the Amalekites is that God was with Israel. The one characteristic of the people of the Lord is "the manifest presence of God."

A flag is also a sign of protection. When soldiers march under the flag of, say, the United States, they affirm that the resources of the United States will be used to defend them. So when we march under the banner of the Lord, we know that He is with us every step of the way. He not only gives us strength for the journey but He protects us, screening us from those encounters He does not want us to experience. Under His banner, we have all the resources for the journey.

When the celebration was over, Moses was told, "Write this in a book as a memorial, and recite it to Joshua, that I will utterly blot out the memory of Amalek from under heaven" (v. 14). Then the Lord added, "I will have war against Amalek from generation to generation" (v. 16). So Moses recorded the details, and this eventually became a part of the Old Testament.

Centuries later Saul was told that he was to exterminate the Amalekites, but his partial obedience led to his downfall. Samuel had told him to "utterly destroy all that he has, and do not spare him; but put to death both man and woman, child and infant, ox and sheep, camel and donkey" (1 Sm 15:3). Saul disobeyed, arguing that he spared the best the Amalekites had to offer. Interestingly, years later when Saul committed suicide, it was an Amalekite who apparently "finished him off" just as he was breathing his last.

The battle with the flesh is one in which there can be no permanent compromise—all temporary compromises will eventually be used by the enemy to increase his grasp. *That which we do not conquer will conquer us.*

How long did it take for Joshua to begin losing the battle when Moses put down his hands? It appears as if the effect was immediate. Victory is ultimately God-given; it must be received by faith through prayer. If not, we are fighting in a battle already lost. Victory is not to be attained, it is to be received.

When you feel the heat in the valley, look to the top of the hill. "Prayer," says Charles Haddon Spurgeon, "pulls the rope down below and the great bell rings above in the ears of God. Some pray so timidly, they scarcely ring the bell ... but he who communicates with heaven is the man who grasps the rope boldly and pulls the rope continuously with all of his might."

Today God is still at war with Amalek. That part of us that is in rebellion against God needs to be subdued. Satan, who seeks to exploit us, needs to be resisted. We must know our enemy and then use our weapons to fight him.

Perhaps today or tomorrow we will come to our Rephidim. Only those who have drawn near to God will win the war.

Just ask Moses.

TEN

When God Comes

(Read Exodus 19–20)

If, as Tozer has said, what we think about God is probably the most important thing about us, our age is in serious trouble. Today, our conceptions of God are, for the most part, made according to our own liking. As Paul taught, we are always faced with the temptation of creating God in our own image.

Opinion polls say that Americans are very religious, but only 10 percent say that their belief in God actually affects the way they live. The god of cultural America is as tolerant as a TV talk-show host, as loving as a doting parent, and as irrelevant as last year's calendar.

Moses would say that if your belief in God does not affect the way you live, you have believed in the wrong god! The God of Abraham, Isaac, and Jacob does not leave those who know Him unaffected. He comes to convict, to convert, and to change the direction of our lives. And sometimes He even causes mountains to quake.

If there was any lesson God wanted Moses and the Israelites to learn, it was that He alone could properly be called *awesome*. There is no one like Him in glory and majesty. Theologians use the word *immanent* to affirm that God is with us in the world and *transcendent* to mean that God is separate from the world. Our age has stressed His immanence, that is, His nearness to us. In drawing near there is a danger that we forget how radically different He is from us.

God is beyond anything we can imagine. When we try to imagine the God who fills the heaven of heavens, we find ourselves at the end of our mental capacities. And yet, only then are we able to enjoy the indescribable grandeur of God. And when we contemplate the holiness of this infinite Being, we kneel in reverence and awe.

The Israelites were three months out of Egypt when they arrived at Mount Sinai to receive the Law. They would learn that though God is everywhere, His presence is usually hidden from us; we see Him only through the eye of faith. But when He reveals Himself, it is breathtaking and frightening.

Read this description of God's revelation on Mount Sinai, trying as best you can to relive the drama that Moses experienced in dialogue with God:

Now Mount Sinai was all in smoke because the Lord descended upon it in fire; and its smoke ascended like the smoke of a furnace, and the whole mountain quaked violently. When the sound of the trumpet grew louder and louder, Moses spoke and God answered him with thunder. And the Lord came down on Mount Sinai, to the top of the mountain; and the Lord called Moses to the top of the mountain, and Moses went up. Then the Lord spoke to Moses, "Go down, warn the people, lest they break through to the Lord to gaze, and many of them perish. And also let the priests who come near to the Lord consecrate themselves, lest the Lord break out against them." And Moses said to the Lord, "The people cannot come up to Mount Sinai, for Thou didst warn us, saying, 'Set bounds about the mountain and consecrate it.'" Then the Lord said to him, "Go down and come up again, you and Aaron with you; but do not let the priests and the people break through to come up to the Lord, lest He break forth upon them." So Moses went down to the people and told them.

EXODUS 19:18-25

What did Moses and Aaron learn about God in this terrifying and humiliating experience? They were brought low before the Almighty in silence and worship. They could never forget God's mercy and His power, His grace and holiness.

What happened when God came to Mount Sinai?

His Holiness Was Revealed

God's most fundamental attribute is holiness. It is the only attribute that is elevated "to the third degree" anywhere in Scripture. We do not read, "powerful, powerful, powerful is the Lord God of Hosts!" But the angels do say, "Holy, holy, holy is the Lord God of Hosts; the whole earth is full of His glory!" (Is 6:3)

Holiness means "otherness." It means that God goes beyond all that we are able to imagine. Holiness is so fundamental to God's character that R.C. Sproul says, "The word *holy* calls attention to all that God is. It reminds us that His love is holy love, His justice is holy justice, His mercy is holy mercy, His knowledge is holy knowledge, His spirit is holy spirit" *(The Holiness of God* [Wheaton, Ill.: Tyndale House], 57).

How did God reveal His holiness at Mount Sinai? First, by insisting that everyone step back from the mountain:

And you shall set bounds for the people all around, saying, "Beware that you do not go up on the mountain or touch the border of it; whoever touches the mountain shall surely be put to death. No hand shall touch him, but he shall surely be stoned or shot through; whether beast or man, he shall not live." When the ram's horn sounds a long blast, they shall come up to the mountain.

EXODUS 19:12-13

If so much as an animal or man touched the mountain, they were not to be retrieved by direct contact but to be shot with an arrow. Moses alone was called to the top of Sinai to see the fire, lightning, and smoke. He then returned to warn the people that they would be struck down if they came close to the mountain.

This physical distance symbolized the moral distance between man and God. We cannot have direct contact with God without a mediator. Not even Moses was able to see God directly, though he was given special privileges. God was saying, "Stay back or be killed!"

In most pagan religions, God is thought of as living in the mountains. But here God is viewed as descending onto the mountain from heaven. There was not just a horizontal distance between God and man but also a vertical distance. God comes down from above as a reminder that man is from below, a creature of the earth.

God is separated; He exceeds the limits. He is greater than His creation and so rises above it. Again Sproul says, "When we meet the Infinite, we become acutely conscious that we are finite. When we meet the Eternal, we know we are temporal. To meet God is a powerful study in contrasts" (p. 63).

Later in Israel's history, two priests named Nadab and Abihu went into the tabernacle and were instantly struck down because they offered "strange fire" to the Lord (Lv 10:2). Apparently they didn't think that their violation was serious. Sure they didn't follow procedures, but everyone has his own rules and serves God in his own way. But whatever they did, God judged them by a quick death.

Did the punishment fit the crime? Of course God did not overreact. When He utters a clear command He expects un-questioned obedience. After all, He not only knows best but is constantly monitoring our allegiance. If the magnitude of a sin is calculated by the greatness of the being against whom it is committed, then these two priests were profoundly guilty. Their disobedience was arrogance. They had profaned that which was holy.

Uzzah, you might recall, was struck down by God for touching the ark of God when it was being brought back to Jerusalem. This wooden chest, which symbolized the presence of God, was put on a new cart with oxen pulling it. When they came to the threshing floor of Chidon, Uzzah reached out his hand to steady the ark because the oxen stumbled. We read, "The Lord's anger burned against Uzzah, and He struck him down because he had put his hand on the ark. So he died there before God. Then David was angry because the Lord's wrath had broken out against Uzzah" (1 Chr 13:10-11, NIV).

Once again we are confronted with the apparent harshness of God. Why should Uzzah be struck down for what was surely an instinctive reaction? The answer is that Uzzah was a Kohathite who had been schooled in specific instructions about how the ark was to be carried. Under no conditions was anyone ever to touch the ark. Once it was constructed and dedicated to God, it was holy. Only the poles could be touched. Actually, the ark should not have even been on an oxcart. When the tabernacle was carried in the wilderness, the ark was covered with the veil in such a way that the priests did not even look upon it.

Uzzah assumed that these instructions could be ignored because the ark was about to fall unto the ground. This was not an act of heroism, but to quote R.C. Sproul once more, "It was an act of arrogance, a sin of presumption. Uzzah assumed that his hand was less polluted than the earth. But it wasn't the ground or the mud that would desecrate the ark; it was the touch of a man.... God did not want His holy throne touched by that which was contaminated by evil, that which was in rebellion to Him.... It was man's touch that was forbidden" (p. 141).

We should not think that God has become more mellow as the ages progress. In the Old Testament there are at least a dozen different sins that demand the death penalty. The list includes the cursing of parents, adultery, and homosexuality. Today, these sins are committed without fear of any such judgment. Is the God of the Old Testament particularly angry and vengeful?

Skeptics such as David Hume argued that there is evolution in our view of God. The God of the Old Testament was vicious, inflicting punishment at a whim, whereas the God of the New Testament is loving and kind. Hume was thankful that our concept of God was becoming more humane.

Why this difference between the Old Testament and the New? The thought that God has changed is blasphemous. As the text of Scripture says, "I am the Lord, I change not." The God of the Old Testament is the God of the New. In this era, however, He has chosen to postpone judgment. Today men and women are given opportunities to repent without the severe immediate judgment rendered in Old Testament times. In the end His holiness and unchangeability will be revealed. Only those who have fled to Christ to be shielded from His wrath will escape the coming judgment.

Today we often emphasize the grace of God. But we cannot understand the wonder of His grace until we are overwhelmed by the blazing intensity of His holiness. To recapture a proper fear of God, we must return to Mount Sinai. We must stand with Moses and see the mountain quake and the fire burn. We must stand with the Israelites at the base of the mountain and see the smoke rise into the air.

How did Moses manage in the presence of God? He returned to the people several times only to return to the top of the mountain again. The first time we read, "And Moses went up to God" (Ex 19:3). Each time he went back up, it appears that his relationship with God became more intimate. After the Law had been given we read, "Moses approached the thick cloud where God was" (20:21). After this, he was asked to come to the top of the mountain for a fifth time, the elders accompanying him to a certain point. But he alone went up to the cloud where he stayed for forty days and forty nights receiving instructions for the tabernacle (24:18). When he returned to the people, he became angry because of their idolatry (to be considered in the next chapter).

When God comes, there is a demonstration of holiness. The closer we get to God, the greater our sins appear. And the greater our sins, the greater our need for His mercy.

His Expectations Were Revealed

We read, "Now Mount Sinai was all in smoke because the Lord descended upon it in fire; and its smoke ascended like the smoke of a furnace, and the whole mountain quaked violently" (19:18).

We can't begin to calculate the power it would take to shake a mountain. Even today, we can see the power of God in tornadoes, hurricanes, and earthquakes. When God wants to shake the earth, He finds no difficulty in doing so. We cannot make a single molecule out of nothing, but God created the stars and planets in a moment of time. The God who created Mount Sinai now shook it.

Now that God had the attention of Moses and the people, He revealed the Ten Commandments. These moral laws reflect God's own character. He began with, "You shall have no other gods before Me" (20:3). Why does God have a right to such allegiance? It's because no other being has intrinsic worth; since all other beings are created by God, their value is derived from their Creator. For us, jealousy is sin because it assumes that we have certain rights or expectations which are being violated. But God alone has intrinsic rights. He is the only one who can receive praise without having to pass it on to a superior. He has every right to be jealous when we have divided loyalties.

The second commandment emphasized that the worship of God was to be spiritual and not material. "You shall not make for yourself an idol, or any likeness of what is in heaven above or on the earth beneath or in the water under the earth" (v. 4). God requires exclusive devotion. Far from aiding worship, any representation detracts from it.

The other commandments will not be given here, except to

say that the first four speak about our relationship to God and the last six about our relationship to others. These commandments were to become the moral foundation of Israel's lifestyle; they represented the most basic code of conduct that God expected.

When God speaks, all arguments end. David Hume believed that it was immoral to believe that God revealed Himself to one people (the Jews) in one geographical area (Israel) through one man (Christ). The problem, of course, is that God did not see the need to run his plans past Hume for approval. "But our God is in the heavens; He does whatever He pleases" (Ps 115:3).

We are accountable to God, not men. Calvin said that we learn to survive by looking around to find someone who is a greater sinner than we are, so that by comparison we appear to be just and upright. Then when we do so much as one good deed, we have the satisfaction of having elevated ourselves to a higher moral plane. We are deceived by this spurt of self-confidence.

The rich young ruler actually believed he had kept the commandments; he had a small view of his sins because he had a small view of God. Luther said that man's problem is not just that he is blind, sick, and dead but that he perceives himself to be able to see, be healthy, and alive.

God's presence strips us of all superficial judgments. Standing before Him we are humiliated, aware of our overwhelming need for mercy. God's presence reveals superficial human judgments for what they are.

A businessman called his pastor and was sobbing so violently that the pastor thought for certain that a tragedy had befallen the family. When the pastor arrived in his friend's office, he was slumped over his desk crying to God for mercy. When the man regained his composure he said, "God has just shown me my heart and it was as if I were looking into the pit of hell!"

What had this man done that was so wicked? He had adjusted some expense accounts in his favor, a small infraction done routinely by businessmen. But in the presence of God, even small sins become big ones. The size of our God determines the size of our sins.

When God comes, there is moral authority. Discussions about right and wrong come to an end. In His presence, the best we can do is to agree completely with our omniscient Creator.

When the people heard the Law they said, "All the words which the Lord has spoken we will do!" (Ex 24:3) We can appreciate their optimism, but shortly afterward they worshiped a golden calf! If they had understood themselves better, they would have cried to God for the strength they needed to live up to even the most basic code of human conduct.

His Grace Was Revealed

When the people saw lightning, thunder, and smoke, they were terrified and begged that Moses speak to them rather than hearing directly from God. "Speak to us yourself and we will listen; but let not God speak to us, lest we die" (20:19). They were filled with the fear of the Lord, but it led them to draw away from Him rather than draw near.

Moses assured the people that there was grace accompanying the revelation of holiness and wrath, "Do not be afraid; for God has come in order to test you, and in order that the fear of Him may remain with you, so that you may not sin" (v. 20). The people then stood at a distance while Moses approached the thick cloud where God was.

Later, God revealed the Book of Leviticus to Moses so that the people might know how they should approach God. They were to bring sacrifices that would put away their sins so that they could approach God. They were right in understanding God's transcendence, but now they also needed to understand His immanence. Yes, the God whose primary attribute is holiness would dwell among them.

Fifteen centuries later, Christ was born in Bethlehem and at the age of thirty appeared on the banks of the Jordan River. John wrote, "And the Word became flesh, and dwelt among us, and we beheld His glory, glory as of the only begotten from the Father, full of grace and truth.... For the law was given through Moses; grace and truth were realized through Jesus Christ" (Jn 1:14, 17).

Moses was the mediator for the Israelites, but Christ is the Mediator for us. They had only a man who interceded for them; we have the God-man whose sacrifice paid the price of our sin. Indeed, even the sins of the Israelites were laid upon Christ; Moses himself was redeemed by the death of Christ on Calvary.

Notice the profound contrast between the experience of Moses on Mount Sinai and our opportunity to come to God in this special era of grace:

For you have not come to a mountain that may be touched and to a blazing fire, and to darkness and gloom and whirl-wind, and to the blast of a trumpet and the sound of words which sound was such that those who heard begged that no further word should be spoken to them. For they could not bear the command, "If even a beast touches the mountain, it will be stoned." And so terrible was the sight, that Moses said, "I am full of fear and trembling." But you have come to Mount Zion and to the city of the living God, the heavenly Jerusalem, and to myriads of angels, to the general assembly and church of the firstborn who are enrolled in heaven, and to God, the Judge of all, and to the spirits of righteous men made perfect, and to Jesus, the Mediator of a New Covenant, and to the sprinkled blood, which speaks better than the blood of Abel.

HEBREWS 12:18-24

There are two mountains, Sinai and Calvary. At Sinai, the Law was given, declaring men to be sinners. At Calvary, someone took our place that we might be freed from the demands of Sinai. Christ is the one Mediator between God and man who has made our approach to God possible. His sprinkled blood, unlike that of sheep and goats, brings us directly into God's presence. This blood appeased the wrath of God; Christ absorbed the blow so that we might be set free.

Mount Sinai says, "Stay away! Don't approach the mountain!" Mount Calvary says, "Come near through the blood of Christ."

Since therefore, brethren, we have confidence to enter the holy place by the blood of Jesus, by a new and living way which He inaugurated for us through the veil, that is, His flesh, and since we have a great priest over the house of God, let us draw near with a sincere heart in full assurance of faith, having our hearts sprinkled clean from an evil conscience and our bodies washed with pure water.

HEBREWS 10:19-22

Has God changed His mind about the hideousness of sin? Not at all. In fact, He will again reveal His holiness in a future day of judgment. And those who do not respond in this era of grace will be under greater condemnation than those who refused to hear the voice of God at Sinai. The author of Hebrews continues:

> See to it that you do not refuse Him who is speaking. For if those did not escape when they refused Him who warned them on earth, much less shall we escape who turn away from Him who warns from heaven. And His voice shook the earth then, but now He has promised, saying, "Yet once more I will shake not only the earth, but also the heaven." And this expression, "Yet once more," denotes the removing of those things which can be shaken, as of created things, in order that those things which cannot be shaken may remain. Therefore, since we receive a kingdom which cannot be shaken, let us show gratitude, by which we may offer to God an acceptable service with reverence and awe; for our God is a consuming fire.
>
> HEBREWS 12:25-29

The greater the invitation of grace the greater the judgment for those who refuse it! The God of Sinai is approachable through Christ. Greater blessings mean greater judgment if we refuse the offer.

We get closer to God by coming first to Sinai; but from Sinai we must flee to Calvary. The Law crushes us, but grace lifts us. The curse for those who disobey the Law can only be lifted by the One who became a curse for us.

When God comes nothing remains the same.

ELEVEN

The High Cost of Idolatry

(Read Exodus 32:1-29)

*L*eadership magazine had a cartoon captioned: "The Lite
Church." The ad read: "24 percent fewer commitments;
home of the 5-percent tithe; the fifteen-minute sermon; the
forty five-minute worship service; we have only 8 commandments (you get to choose); we have an eight hundred-year
millennium and only three of the four spiritual laws." The bottom line: *All you have ever wanted in a church, and less!*

When Moses was on the top of Mount Sinai receiving the
commandments, the people were in the valley breaking them.
Moses had disappeared and they felt abandoned by God. Their
patience had run out and it was time to take matters into their
own hands.

If the God they had come to know was not at their beck and
call, they would make a god who was. So they chose to fashion
a god who resembled one of the deities they remembered from
their days in Egypt. Then they worshiped in grand style.

When God is silent and appears indifferent to our needs, a
climate is created where idolatry flourishes. Where we turn
when we are desperate speaks volumes about where we are in
our walk with God. Whether we draw closer to God or turn
away from Him depends on how well we know Him. When we
feel that God has failed, an idol stands ready to deliver us. The
closer we are to God the closer we want to get; the farther we

are from Him the more attractive idols become.

We are all idol lovers. Left to ourselves, we drift toward idolatry; we all want to create gods who are according to our liking. Let's not read this story as if it were ancient history. This is a diagnosis of the human heart. When we see the Israelites at the base of the mountain, we see ourselves.

Let's walk through this passage and observe the five stages of an idol lover. At every point, we will take the time to see our reflection in a mirror.

We Fashion Our Idols

When a groundswell of popular support arose asking Aaron to make a god, he probably was appalled. He thought that the people would drop the idea once they understood how much it would cost them. So he made a request: "Tear off the gold rings which are in the ears of your wives, your sons, and your daughters, and bring them to me" (Ex 32:2). To his surprise, the people responded. He had put his foot into a river that was now at high tide, so he felt that there was little he could do but go ahead with their request.

He put the gold in the fire, then took his graving tool and fashioned a calf patterned after the Egyptian bull god Apis, the god of strength and fertility. This, he thought, would be the best representation of the Lord God; what is more, it was a replica of the kind of god the people had become accustomed to.

Bear in mind that Aaron probably did not think of this idol as a substitute for Jehovah. He knew very well that this physical object could not be credited with the miracles the people had seen in Egypt and the wilderness. Even today when the heathen bow to idols, they do not worship the physical form but the unseen spiritual power it represents.

Further evidence that Aaron did not want to give credit to a golden calf is found in his proclamation, "Tomorrow shall be a feast to the Lord" (v. 5). Apparently, in his mind this bull was only a representation of Jehovah, the Lord God. It was only a "worship helper," a role that many people give to statues today.

Idolatry can sprout in the most unlikely conditions. One day the Israelites were grumbling about the food God had given them in the wilderness, so God sent "fiery serpents" among them. These bit the people and many died. They begged Moses to intercede for them. God graciously responded by asking Moses to make a bronze serpent and put it on a high pole. Whoever looked at that serpent was healed (Nm 21:6-9).

Centuries later, that bronze snake turned up on a hilltop as an idol with a special name. When Hezekiah removed the places of idol worship, he also "broke in pieces the bronze serpent that Moses had made, for until those days the sons of Israel burned incense to it; and it was called Nehushtan" (2 Kgs 18:4). For more than seven centuries they had revered the bronze serpent and actually worshiped it. How easily idolatry flourishes within the human heart.

Regardless of Aaron's rationalizations, he was breaking the first commandment, "You shall have no other gods before Me." And he most assuredly was breaking the second commandment.

You shall not make for yourself an idol, or any likeness of what is in heaven above or on the earth beneath or in the water under the earth. You shall not worship them or serve them; for I, the Lord your God, am a jealous God, visiting the iniquity of the fathers on the children, on the third and the fourth generations of those who hate Me, but showing loving-kindness to thousands, to those who love Me and keep My commandments.

EXODUS 20:4-6

In ancient times idols were made by human hands; in our day they are usually conceived in the human mind. Our ideas of God in America and Canada have been grossly tainted by our culture. We all are tempted to make God into the being we want Him to be. Idolatry is motivated by an unholy ambition; in our day it is not so much abandoning God as the arrogant notion that we can reshape Him so that He will be more in tune with our culture.

Julian Huxley admitted in a television interview, "The reason we accepted Darwinism without a lot of scientific proof is because we did not want to have God interfere with our sexual mores." There you have it: We want a God who will let us do whatever we want! We do not want to bend toward God, we want a god who will bend toward us. Even a redefinition of God, based on our own understanding, is idolatry.

It is even more subtle. Many of us are not tempted to worship evil things, but we are tempted to put God second to good things. Since idolatry is anything that stands between us and God, there can be as many idols as there are consuming interests among us.

An idol can be a person, a place, or a dream that we want even more than God's will. An idol can be any legitimate desire that we insist is ours whether it is God's will for us or not. Idols need only divert our affections from the living God. Usually, idolatry is nothing more than putting ourselves in first place.

Identifying our idols is quite easy. We must ask two questions: What do we think about in our spare time? And, whom do we wish to please? C.S. Lewis said that our idol is simply our "overwhelming first."

Stage One in our slide toward idolatry is to cherish something more than the true God. We fashion a god according to our liking. Once we have chosen our idol we bow in worship.

We Worship Our Idols

Every God demands allegiance. Not only had the people given up their gold to construct the golden calf, but now more was demanded. They brought costly sacrifices so that their worship might be accepted. We read, "So the next day they rose early and offered burnt offerings, and brought peace offerings; and the people sat down to eat and to drink, and rose up to play" (32:6).

Our idols are hungry for power and recognition; they will take anything they can from us. The goal of every god is control. Either we will be owned by the living and true God or else we will be owned by an idol. Either way, we are not our own; the gods rule us.

Worshiping an idol is not difficult in the early stages of commitment. For now the Israelites were able to pay what the idol demanded. Later, when they entered the land and adopted the pagan practices of the Canaanites, they were required to sacrifice their children to the gods of the land. So today: Our initial flirtation with the goddess of sexual immorality might have appeared harmless, but today that goddess demands the sacrifice of millions of unborn babies every year.

At first, pagan gods seem easily appeased, but later they demand increasing allegiance. The *stimulation* comes first, *the strangulation* comes later. Every god seeks to control us.

We Enjoy Our Idols

The Israelites had a sexual orgy in the presence of their newly minted god. Here is Paul's comment on this incident: "And do not be idolaters, as some of them were; as it is written, 'The people sat down to eat and drink, and stood up to play.' Nor let us act immorally, as some of them did, and twenty-three thousand fell in one day" (1 Cor 10:7-8).

Interestingly, once they had changed their god, they began to behave differently; they behaved just as their god would have wanted them to (for all the gods of Egypt were tolerant of sexual freedom). Sacrificing their jewelry had paid off, for they now had a tame god who had a better understanding of their needs and weaknesses. Idolatry has its perks.

How do we enjoy our idols today? First, our idolatry enables us to serve ourselves while claiming to serve God. Our consumer-oriented society has remodeled our idea of God to conform to what we would like God to be. God, rather than judging culture, has become more like the cultural products of convenience and consumerism. There is a distinct possibility that our culture will devour religion. Or to put it differently, our religion is becoming indistinguishable from our culture.

Second, when we worship one idol, we soon become tolerant of other idols. Finite gods are always indulgent, tolerant of our behavior, and accepting of one another. The reason the New Age movement is open to absurd and contradictory beliefs is that it has no objective standard by which truth can be judged. Idol worshipers enjoy the company of other idol worshipers no matter what those idols be.

Now that the Israelites had chosen to worship the golden calf, the next step would have been to include other gods in their worship. Once the principle was accepted that gods existed to let people enjoy themselves, there was no limit either to the number of gods or the experiences that could be explored. Only the intervention of Moses prevented the next step.

We Are Fooled by Our Idols

God told Moses about the idolatry of the people and asked him to go down and take care of the crisis. In fact, God was so angry he said to Moses, "Now then let Me alone, that My anger may burn against them, and I will destroy them; and I will make of you a great nation" (Ex 32:10).

Then Moses turned and went down from the mountain with the two tablets of testimony in his hand, tablets which were written on both sides. These were God's work, His own writing was engraved on the stone. "Now when Joshua heard the sound of the people as they shouted, he said to Moses, 'There is a sound of war in the camp.' But he said, 'It is not the sound of the cry of triumph, nor is it the sound of the cry of defeat; but the sound of singing I hear.' And it came about, as soon as Moses came near the camp, that he saw the calf and the dancing" (vv. 17-19). When he realized that the nation was out of control, he became so angry he threw the two tablets down and they lay shattered on the ground before him. This was a symbol of what the nation had just done. What he had done physically, they had done morally and spiritually.

And he took the calf which they had made and burned it with fire, and ground it to powder, and scattered it over the surface of the water, and made the sons of Israel drink it. Then Moses said to Aaron, "What did this people do to you, that you have brought such great sin upon them?" And Aaron said, "Do not let the anger of my lord burn; you know the people yourself, that they are prone to evil. For they said to me, 'Make a god for us who will go before us; for this Moses, the man who brought us up from the land of Egypt, we do not know what has become of him.' And I said to them, 'Whoever has any gold, let them tear it off.' So they gave it to me, and I threw it into the fire, and out came this calf."

EXODUS 32:20-24

How did Aaron react? First he blamed the people and then he blamed the furnace. He threw the gold into the fire and the calf just walked out of the flames. If it weren't for these fancy furnaces in the desert, things like this would never happen!

Moses was dumbfounded when he saw that his people would deviate so quickly from the pure worship of God. He had just been face to face with God; now he was face to face with sin. He could scarcely bear the contrast.

Making them drink the water sprinkled with gold dust was just a part of their judgment. Their god was humiliated before their eyes as they had to drink the bitter potion. Whatever promises the people thought they had extracted from this object, in a moment of crisis he simply did not come through. This god could not defend himself from destruction. In the end, idols simply do not keep their promises. Idolatry is deception.

Yes, our idols deceive us. The marriage we wanted so badly that we did not even ask God for His wisdom, turns into a nightmare. The promotion we manipulated is fraught with compromises and distress. And the value of real estate we bought to get rich plummets before our eyes. Try as we might, our god will eventually lose its luster.

God never lets us get by with idolatry. Either in this life or the life to come, we will see clearly that our gods will fail us. God hates idolatry.

We Must Repent of Our Idols

Moses and Aaron are a study in contrasts. Moses, through his association with God, had largely become immune to public opinion. His overarching desire to obey God gave him the courage needed to override the opinions of the multitudes.

Aaron, on the other hand, simply did not have the inner fortitude to withstand public sentiment. He was sensitive to the political implications of popular opinion and didn't have the heart to tell the people what they needed to hear.

If we find this evasion of responsibility strange, let us remember that the devil has an excuse for every sin we are willing to commit! Either we convince ourselves that what God says is sin really isn't, or we blame someone else. Or perhaps responsibility rests with the furnace that creates these idols on its own!

Interestingly, Moses wasn't impressed with the story. Nor was he sympathetic because he had been gone for forty days and forty nights without giving an explanation to the people. Nothing can justify idolatry.

Now when Moses saw that the people were out of control—for Aaron had let them get out of control to be a derision among their enemies—then Moses stood in the gate of the camp, and said, "Whoever is for the Lord, come to me!" And all the sons of Levi gathered together to him. And he said to them, "Thus says the Lord, the God of Israel, 'Every man of you put his sword upon his thigh, and go back and forth from gate to gate in the camp, and kill every man his brother, and every man his friend, and every man his neighbor.'" So the sons of Levi did as Moses instructed, and about three thousand men of the people fell that day. Then Moses said, "Dedicate yourselves today to the Lord—for every man has been against his son and against his brother—in order that He may bestow a blessing upon you today."

EXODUS 32:25-29

Why were so many killed? Because some evidently continued in their rebellion even after Moses had come down from the mountain to restore order. Some people repented of their sin. others did not.

How Can We Repent of Our Idols?

Once we have identified our idols, we should name them to God, one by one. Like pulling the weeds in a garden, our work is never finished. After the weeding takes place, we find that new weeds have sprouted; those that we think we have dug up by the roots appear once more. Luther said that the Christian life was one of continual repentance.

We must replace those idols with devotion to Christ. Our souls abhor a vacuum. We need some reason to live; some reason to hope. Either we worship the true God or we worship an idol. Everyone needs an "overwhelming first."

We might think that we are unable to turn from those idols that have ensnared us. But we must turn our focus to God and the idol will eventually lose its power. To the people of Thessalonica Paul wrote, "You turned to God from idols to serve a living and true God" (1 Thes 1:9).

By nature, we are idol lovers. God, by nature, is an idol hater. Whenever we try to coexist with idols, we grieve His Spirit. "To put ourselves in second place," someone has observed, "is the significance of life." And, "to know what to put in first place, is the essence of life."

Idolatry is always practiced at high cost. Idols might promise like a god, but they pay like a devil.

The dearest idol I have known,
What e'er that idol be,
Help me to snatch it from the throne
And worship only Thee.

If we are repentant of our idolatry, God will help us.

TWELVE

A Glimpse of God's Glory

(Read Exodus 32:30-35; 33)

Incredibly, Moses got to see the glory of God. Though we cannot see God as Moses did, we shall discover that we too can see His glory in a different way. Reliving this event with Moses will whet our appetite for getting closer to God than we have ever been before.

To understand this story, we must begin with a question that we've all asked about prayer. Why should we bother to pray when everything is already in God's hands? If He chooses to bless our friends, He can do it without our prayers. If He wishes to free the city of Chicago from Satan's oppression, He can do it whether we pray about it or not. He can heal the sick, supply money for missionaries, give us guidance, and promote His cause quite apart from our asking. It would be ludicrous to think that God is somehow bound by our own faithfulness in intercession. We might be tempted to stop praying and just let God do whatever He wishes on earth as He does in heaven.

Why then do we have to pray? The answer is that *prayer is a stepping-stone that leads to a higher objective.* In prayer we come to God with our need, and we soon realize that we need God more than we need an answer to our prayers! Prayer pushes us toward intimacy with the Almighty. He gives us many needs because He knows that only desperate people pray. And the more we pray, the closer we get to Him.

George MacDonald, who greatly influenced C.S. Lewis, said,

What if the main object in God's idea of prayer be the supplying of our great, our endless need of Himself? Hunger may drive a runaway child home, but he needs his mother more than he does his dinner. Communion with God is the one need of the soul beyond all other needs. Prayer is the beginning of that communion (*George MacDonald: An Anthology* [New York: Macmillan, 1948], 51–52).

This explains why we have to pray about our marriage and our vocation; this is why we need to pray about our health. This is why some people don't treat us with the kindness we believe we deserve. Life is hard so that we might lean more desperately on God. We can even live with unanswered prayer, as long as the needs of our soul are satisfied. God always leads us beyond our initial requests to see the bigger picture. The goal is always that we might get closer to Him.

We've learned that when Moses was on Mount Sinai, he was told about the idolatry that was happening in the valley. The people had made a golden calf and were worshiping it. Moses was appalled, for he had seen God at close range; he knew both the beauty and holiness of the Almighty. He knew that idolatry was the ultimate rebellion; it was an inexcusable insult.

God gave Moses this test: "Now then let Me alone, that My anger may burn against them and that I may destroy them; and I will make of you a great nation" (Ex 32:10). Would Moses, who often struggled with anger, agree to this suggestion? The people certainly deserved little better than death; and if God were to start over with Moses and his family, he would stand at the head of a whole new nation.

Moses wouldn't hear of it. His anger was tempered with mercy. And more importantly, he was more concerned about God's reputation than his own place in history. Through his prayer, we are introduced to three levels of praying that should be a part of our own experience. As we grow in our faith, we can graduate from one level of praying to another.

The Prayer for Pardon

Moses began by asking that God might forgive the sin of the nation. He appealed to God's reputation:

> O, Lord why doth Thine anger burn against Thy people whom Thou hast brought out from the land of Egypt with great power and with a mighty hand? Why should the Egyptians speak, saying, "With evil intent He brought them out to kill them in the mountains and to destroy them from the face of the earth." Turn from Thy burning anger and change Thy mind about doing harm to Thy people.
>
> EXODUS 32:11-12

"What will the Egyptians think?" Moses asked. The pagans of his day would misread God's actions. They would scoff at God and conclude that He could not take care of His own people. The reputation of God would be tarnished. Moses wanted the nations to be impressed with God rather than belittle His intentions and power. So he asked God to turn from his burning anger and change His mind about blotting out the people.

Of course, that's the same today. The impression that some people have of God is dependent upon the lifestyle of His followers. Many people will make up their minds about God based on the way we live. We can either represent God as faithful or *mis*represent Him as unfaithful. Our world desperately needs people whose lives radiate the message that God can be trusted.

Remember God told David that his sin had "caused the enemies of the Lord to blaspheme." Scoffers heard about David's sin and ridiculed his profession of faith in God. They no doubt also felt more comfortable with their own sin knowing that one of God's servants had committed adultery and murder.

Moses was jealous for the way God would be perceived by the surrounding nations. They did not want to believe that Israel was a chosen nation; if Israel were now destroyed, the pagans would be sure that the God of Israel was weak and untrustworthy. What nation would want to adopt the God whose people had been wiped off the face of the earth? What would the destruction of the nation say about His integrity? If God did not keep His covenant to those He called His own, they would be betrayed. Moses, in effect, said, "You *can't* blot these people out!"

The next day Moses continued to intercede for the people and prayed, "But now if Thou wilt, forgive their sin—and if not, please blot me out from Thy book which Thou has written" (v. 32).

Moses did not finish the sentence. "Yet now, if Thou wilt forgive their sin—." F.B. Meyer says,

> He could not trust himself to depict the blessed consequences that would ensue if only God would forgive. If Thou wilt forgive, freely, and without a ransom price, then thy noblest attributes will appear; then my tongue shall sing

aloud of the goodness; then I will bind myself to the service with new enthusiasm; then the people surely will become touched with the passion of gratitude and love *(Moses* [Grand Rapids, Mich.: Zondervan], 131).

But if God was unwilling to forgive their sin, Moses was ready to give his own life on their behalf. He says, in effect, "Oh, God, forgive their sin, and if not strike me dead!" He was willing to offer himself as a sin offering on those mountain heights. When he invites God to blot him out of "the book of life," I do not believe that this is the Book of Life which is referred to in the New Testament. Very probably it refers to the census that contained the names of all those who had left Egypt and were headed for the Promised Land. This was the "book of the living." The people had no idea of the price Moses was willing to pay that they might be spared.

Think of what such devotion meant to God! The offer was not accepted, of course. For one thing, no mere human being can die for his own sin much less for the sin of another. For another thing, God had to fulfill the promises He had made and maintain at least a remnant of the twelve sons of Jacob.

God answered Moses' prayer for pardon. Yes, some of the rebels would be put to death, but the nation would stay intact. And with their sins forgiven, they could resume their journey to Canaan (vv. 32-35).

Prayer for forgiveness represents the first steps in our walk with God. Many Christians speak to God only when there is some sin that troubles their conscience. God exists only to wipe the slate clean. He does that, of course, but that is only a small part of the story.

Moses then moves on to a deeper relationship.

Prayer for the Presence of God

Though God answered Moses' prayer for forgiveness, He told him that He (the Lord) would no longer accompany the people of Israel but would send a substitute. "And I will send an angel before you and I will drive out the Canaanite, the Amorite, the Hittite, the Perizzite, the Hivite and the Jebusite" (33:2). God would be with them in the sense that He is everywhere, but the cloud that symbolized His presence would vanish and in its place an angel would be sent to drive out the Canaanites from the land. This was a bitter disappointment because the presence of the Almighty was to be the one distinguishing mark of the people of God.

Moses was dissatisfied. He wanted the cloud of glory to come back to the tent to lead the people. So he prayed, "Now therefore, I pray Thee, if I have found favor in Thy sight, let me know Thy ways, that I may know Thee, so that I may find favor in Thy sight. Consider too, that this nation is Thy people" (v. 13). Moses appealed to his strong desire to know God more personally. Without the cloud he might make it to the Promised Land, but the joy of fellowship would be lost. Moses longed for the companionship of God.

Once again God answered Moses' prayer. "My presence shall go with you, and I will give you rest" (v. 14). This was not the rest of Canaan, which Moses did not see in his earthly existence, but the rest that comes to all those who wait on God. Moses answered, "If Thy presence does not go with us, do not lead us up from here. For how then can it be known that I have found favor in Thy sight, I and Thy people? Is it not by Thy going with us, so that we, I and Thy people, may be distinguished from all the other people who are upon the face of the earth?" (vv. 15-16) God said, in effect, "Since you want My presence so desperately, the cloud of glory will return."

Moses insisted on the necessity of God's presence. If God was not going to send His cloud of glory, Moses was not going to go. No place can satisfy without God; no wealth can satisfy without God; no pleasure can satisfy without God. *Better the desert with God than Canaan without Him!*

What effect would God's presence have? The people would experience what others can only imagine, namely, "the manifest presence of God." His nearness would set the nation apart for special blessing. No matter what would happen, they could look at the cloud and know that God was with them every step of the way.

God never abandons His people, but there are times when He withdraws our conscious enjoyment of His love. Our sin mars our fellowship, grieves the Holy Spirit, and makes us feel that we have been abandoned to our own ways. We then either return to God in confession or follow at a distance.

Do we share the craving Moses had for God's presence? Do we pray, saying in effect, "God, if You cannot bless my plans with Your presence, then I'm not going to fulfill them"? Or might we be tempted to fulfill our own agenda whether God is in our plans or not? Moses knew, even as we should, that there can be no joy where God's presence is not evident.

So far, Moses uttered two prayers and the Lord answered both of them. You would think he would be satisfied. After all, what else can one ask? The people were forgiven and the cloud representing God's presence was restored to the nation. It was time to get on with the business of moving ahead toward the Promised Land.

But Moses is still dissatisfied. He makes a third request, which leads us to the heart of what prayer is all about.

The Person of God

Moses now graduates to the highest level of praying. "And the Lord said to Moses, 'I will also do this thing of which you have spoken; for you have found favor in My sight, and I have known you by name.' Then Moses said, 'I pray Thee, show me Thy glory!'" (vv. 17-18).

This is the Moses who had just been on the mountain with God; this is the Moses about whom we read, "Thus the Lord used to speak to Moses face to face, just as a man speaks to his friend" (v. 11). Here is a man who could commune with God and have an immediate answer. He had privileges no other man could claim. Yet, though he had enjoyed God's company on a one-on-one basis, he still has not had enough! He is asking for more of God. He is saying, "O God, show me as much of You as I am able to take!"

"And [the Lord] said, 'I Myself will make all My goodness pass before you, and will proclaim the name of the Lord before you; and I will be gracious to whom I will be gracious, and will show compassion on whom I will show compassion.' But He said, 'You cannot see My face, for no man can see Me and live!'" (vv. 19-20) To see God directly would be like standing next to the sun. Obviously Moses would be consumed. He had just made an impossible request.

Or had he? Although no one can see God directly, it is possible to see a manifestation of God. Let me ask: Have you seen your face today? The answer is both yes and no. Yes, we have all seen our faces in a mirror, but of course not a one of us has ever seen his or her face directly.

Moses' faith grew bolder with each request.

God accommodated Himself to Moses' deep desire. He said,

Behold there is a place by Me, and you shall stand there on the rock; and it will come about, while My glory is passing by, that I will put you in the cleft of the rock and cover you with My hand until I have passed by. Then I will take My hand away and you shall see My back but My face shall not be seen.

EXODUS 33:21-23

So Moses is granted this third request. He will receive a special revelation of the beauty of God. The very presence of God will pass by him and he will be able to get another glimpse of God's glory. The glory of God is the sum of His attributes; it is God's beauty and goodness.

What did this experience mean? First, Moses was privy to *further intimacy* with God. God had said, "I have known you by name." And now He turns to Moses and says, "I will declare My name unto you." Just think of the beauty in that relationship. Just as God knows Moses, Moses is going to be led to a deeper relationship with God.

Is it biblical to say that we can be on a first-name basis with God? That depends on how that expression is understood. If we mean that we are equals, the answer is no. But if we mean that we can be a friend of God and speak to Him directly and hear Him respond from His Word, the answer is yes. We can call Him "Abba! Father!"

As a part of this new understanding, Moses will experience the grace of God. The Lord says, "I will be gracious ... and show compassion on whom I will show compassion" (v. 19). Literally that word *compassion* means that God "bends toward human need." The manifestation of God's presence passing by Moses was a beautiful example of God's extraordinary love for His servant.

Second, Moses experienced the *transformation* of God. When he came down from the mountain, his face shone though he was not conscious of it. "And it came about when Moses was coming down from Mount Sinai (and the two tablets of the testimony were in Moses' hand as he was coming down from the mountain), that Moses did not know that the skin of his face shone because of his speaking with Him" (34:29). Even his brother Aaron was afraid to come near him.

Later when Moses went into the "tent of meeting," the people gathered to behold the cloud of glory descend. There in God's presence, Moses would take the veil off, but when he came out he would put it on so the people would not have to look at a glory which would eventually fade. Those who spend time with the Almighty reflect the glory of God on their faces, but they are not aware of it.

When I make an effort to be humble, I have not yet attained humility. Unconscious godliness has the fragrance of God, whereas self-conscious godliness has the stench of hypocrisy. True godliness cannot be manufactured; it is something we must let God do for us. Unconscious godliness reflects the work of God in the soul. An old legend says that saints who meditate long on the crucifixion of the Lord receive in their very flesh the marks of His wounds.

Just as the moon has no light of itself but simply reflects the sun, so we can be objects of God's light and beauty. We can show to men and women the worth of God by the way we live and by what we say.

When we've been with God, we are different—our morals, moods, desires, and goals change. We face life with courage and optimism because we know God. And the better we know Him the greater our appetite for further fellowship.

Does Moses finally have his soul satisfied? Yes, but he still wants more. In fact, even after he dies and is buried by God, he wants more of the Almighty. Fifteen centuries later, he is still enjoying the glory of God.

Moses was barred from entering the land because of his disobedience (to be discussed in the next chapter). Yet, he does get to enter the land after all! Christ asked Peter, James, and John to come with Him to the top of a mountain. "And He was transfigured before them; and His face shone like the sun, and His garments became white as light" (Mt 17:2). And who should appear at this historic meeting but Moses and Elijah!

Not only had Moses finally entered the land, but he had received another revelation of the glory of God. The man who had prayed centuries earlier, "Show me Thy glory," was not yet satisfied and God gave him a further answer to his prayer.

Some of our prayers will not be completely fulfilled in this life, but will be more finally realized in the future. Moses could not have dreamed that his prayer would be answered in such a dramatic way and so far into the future. Even today he still is delighting in God's glory, and someday we will be invited to join him in such glad worship.

Our Opportunity to See Glory

We might be tempted to think, "How fortunate Moses was to see a display of God's glory!" We might actually regret living in this age when God doesn't speak to us directly. We might find ourselves wishing that we lived back in those Old Testament times when the mountains shook and the cloud appeared. Or perhaps we nostalgically wish we had been living when Christ was on earth, so that we could have seen Him directly.

We must put an end to such daydreams. The glorious fact is that we are living in an era that has greater opportunities for us than for those who lived in biblical times. True, Moses had special privileges, but the masses of people had to stay away from the mountain. In contrast, today all believers enjoy the privileges which in Moses' day were limited to a few.

Paul agreed that the ministry of Moses was glorious, but then he contrasts those days and ours: "But we all, with unveiled face beholding as in a mirror the glory of the Lord, are being transformed into the same image from glory to glory, just as from the Lord, the Spirit" (2 Cor 3:18). As the spirit surpasses the letter and as the table of the heart is better than the table of stone, so the ministry of grace supersedes the ministry of Moses which was characterized by law.

We have a *greater opportunity*—"we all." In the Old Testament God asked people to stay away—they were to stay away from Mount Sinai and stay away from the holy of holies. As mentioned, only the representatives of the nation could draw near and even they did so in fear. Today, thanks to the work of Christ on the cross, all are invited to come. "Since therefore, brethren, we have confidence to enter the holy place by the blood of Jesus ... let us draw near with a sincere heart in full assurance of faith, having our hearts sprinkled clean from an evil conscience and our bodies washed with pure water" (Heb 10:19-22).

Second, we also have *greater boldness*, for we can come "with unveiled face." Moses veiled himself because he did not want the people to see that the glory of his face would eventually fade. The veil was a reminder of the temporary nature of his experience. We behold the glory of the Lord with unveiled face because our acceptance with Him is complete and permanent. We can come to God just as we are, based on the blood of Christ.

Third, we see with *greater clarity*—"beholding as in a mirror the glory of the Lord." In the Old Testament they saw the glory of God as though looking into water. Christ was depicted in types and shadows, but when He actually came He brought God to us with clarity. John wrote, "For the Law was given through Moses; grace and truth were realized through Jesus Christ. No man has seen God at any time; the only begotten God, who is in the bosom of the Father, He has explained Him" (Jn 1:17-18). Christ has come, the Word of God is complete, and we can see the glory of God.

Finally, for us there is a *greater transformation*. We are "transformed from glory into glory even as by the Spirit of the Lord." The work God does in our hearts continues in this life and will continue until we see Christ face to face. In the Old Testament the ministry of the Spirit was limited in extent (not all people were indwelt) and in duration (the Spirit did not abide permanently). Christ explained our greater advantage: "And I will ask the Father, and He will give you another Helper, that He may be with you forever" (14:16).

Some people are satisfied simply with God's *pardon*, which emphasizes the *gifts* of God. Others progress to a desire for *His presence*, which emphasizes the *guidance* of God. Like Moses, they say "Unless Your presence goes with me I will not go." But then there are others, possibly only a few, who press to the highest intimacy and seek a glimpse of the *glory* of God. Those people discover the true purpose of prayer.

We are invited to pray, not just to get our needs met but to understand that our greatest need is for God Himself. Our needs set us to praying; our prayers set us to worshiping. And once we are satisfied with Him, everything else tends to fall together for the glory of the Lord.

C.S. Lewis said that God is the "all-satisfying object." We come because we are hungry, but we need our Father more than we need our supper! The closer we get, the closer we want to come.

"Lord, show me Thy glory!"

THIRTEEN

Failure and Hope
at the Finish Line

(Read Numbers 20)

Wouldn't it be wonderful if Christians never failed? Think of what it would be like if we never lost our temper, made unwise investments, or made foolish promises! Yet we all know someone who has failed miserably through moral indiscretion, dishonesty, and hatred. Failure of some kind is common to us all.

Even Moses failed near the end of his distinguished career. To understand the details, we must recap an incident that happened nearly forty years earlier at the beginning of the wilderness journeys. A few weeks into the wilderness, the congregation became angry because there was no water to drink. They not only blamed Moses but quarreled with him, accusing him of bringing them into the wilderness to let them die of thirst. He even thought they might stone him. When he cried to God, he received these instructions: "'Behold, I will stand before you there on the rock at Horeb; and you shall strike the rock, and water will come out of it, that the people may drink.' And Moses did so in the sight of the elders of Israel" (Ex 17:6).

This rod which he had acquired during his humiliating days in Midian reminded him of his special assignment and it also was a symbol of power. We can only imagine the elation that swept through the crowd when water flowed. Moses' own confidence grew as he saw the faithfulness of God before his very eyes. But because the people had tested the Lord there, Moses gave the place two names—Massah ("testing") and Meribah ("quarreling").

After spending two years at Mount Sinai, the people went to Kadesh Barnea to spy out the land God had given them. Unfortunately, ten of the twelve spies brought back a frightening report about walled cities, giants, and high hills. The news spread unbelief throughout the camp and God was displeased. Moses pled for the people and God chose to forgive their sin but also gave them a stern judgment: The nation would have to wander in the desert another thirty-eight years, long enough for the whole generation of adults to die. Only the children and their descendants would enter the land.

Now we must fast-forward to the end of the forty-year period when the nation was preparing to cross over the Jordan. Once again, the congregation angrily contended with Moses because they were thirsty. Moses spoke to God and he was told to get water from the stream beside the rock. Only this time he was only to *speak* to the rock, not strike it. Read the account:

And there was no water for the congregation; and they assembled themselves against Moses and Aaron. The people thus contended with Moses and spoke, saying, "If only we had perished when our brothers perished before the Lord! Why then have you brought the Lord's assembly into this wilderness, for us and our beasts to die here? And why have you made us come up from Egypt, to bring us in to this wretched place? It is not a place of grain or figs or vines or pomegranates, nor is there water to drink." Then Moses and Aaron came in from the presence of the assembly to the doorway of the tent of meeting, and fell on their faces. Then the glory of the Lord appeared to them; and the Lord spoke to Moses, saying, "Take the rod; and you and your brother Aaron assemble the congregation and speak to the rock before their eyes, that it may yield its water. You shall thus bring forth water for them out of the rock and let the congregation and their beasts drink." So Moses took the rod from before the Lord, just as He had commanded him; and Moses and Aaron gathered the assembly before the rock. And he said to them, "Listen now, you rebels; shall we bring forth water for you out of this rock?" Then Moses lifted up his hand and struck the rock twice with his rod; and water came forth abundantly, and the congregation and their beasts drank. But the Lord said to Moses and Aaron, "Because you have not believed Me, to treat Me as holy in the sight of the sons of Israel, therefore you shall not bring this assembly into the land which I have given them." Those were the waters of Meribah, because the sons of Israel contended with the Lord, and He proved Himself holy among them.

NUMBERS 20:2-13

Obviously, Moses had failed. In anger he disobeyed the precise instructions the Lord had given. And the consequences were more severe than he could ever have imagined.

Let's consider this mistake from three perspectives:

Moses' Perspective

No doubt Moses felt quite justified in losing his temper. In fact, hitting the rock might have felt good; it was an emotional release he thought he needed. He might well have still been nursing an old wound.

Back in Egypt, eighty years earlier, he had risked frequent walks to monitor the plight of these slaves and had been rejected. Killing the Egyptian was another risk he was willing to take for their good. When it backfired, he felt deeply hurt and rejected again. That emotional scar took a long while to heal.

Then for forty years he was battered by the complaints of the people whose loyalty vanished with every passing trial. He had grown tired of their anger and false accusations. This time the attack was especially vicious. They assailed his motives, saying that he had brought them into the desert to die there. "And why have you made us come up from Egypt, to bring us in to this wretched place? It is not a place of grain or figs or vines or pomegranates, nor is there water to drink" (v. 5). Of course the desert did not have fruit and grain! This was a description of the Promised Land, not the hot, arid Sinai Peninsula!

What must have particularly hurt Moses was the sad realization that this new generation was no better than the old one which had almost died out. The children were acting like their parents. If the old generation died under the judgment of God, what hope was there for this new generation that was repeating the same sins? This was the reward for his faithful leadership?

We can see ourselves in this story. Many of us have experienced disappointment in our walk with God, complaining that it is not everything that the New Testament makes it out to be. We hear about others who experience the strength of Christ, but we feel cheated, unfulfilled, and spiritually dry. The reason, of course, is that we have not made the promises ours; we have not stood with Christ to take territory from the enemy.

Moses had had enough. He took the rod as God had commanded, but as God had *not* commanded he struck the rock twice and the water flowed. As the stream gushed out, Moses very probably saw this miracle as confirmation that his anger was justified.

But there was another side to the story.

The Congregation's Perspective

What did the congregation think of Moses' smiting the rock? They were indifferent to his angry outburst. For one thing, they probably did not know that he had disobeyed God. It is unlikely that Moses would tell the people, "God asked me to speak to the rock, but I'm going to hit it!" The masses were not privy to the fact that their leader was failing a crucial test.

Regardless, the congregation was delighted that the water flowed. The stream was so abundant that all the people and the cattle drank. When you are about to die of dehydration and you get water, you are not concerned about the details. If smiting the rock worked, what could be wrong with it? Why be concerned about a technicality?

Leaders must learn that the masses want results at any cost. In America, we are told, "People vote with their pocketbook." The morality of their leader, the wisdom of his economic theories, or even his expertise in foreign affairs is not what wins elections. Even if money is borrowed from future generations, the present generation wants what it wants and it wants it now. The how is not important, the what is.

Blessed is the leader who can rule on the basis of principle rather than results. Present results are important, but so are future consequences. Moses was learning.

God's Perspective

God looked at the whole matter differently: "But the Lord said to Moses and Aaron, 'Because you have not believed Me, to treat Me as holy in the sight of the sons of Israel, therefore you shall not bring this assembly into the land which I have given them'" (Nm 20:12).

Notice how God saw this disobedience. He says that Moses did not believe Him; unbelief mistreats the Almighty by questioning whether He is worthy to be obeyed. Unbelief is disrespectful to the holy character of God. What appeared to be a minor infraction to men was a serious breach of honor to God. Since God was with him, the *words* Moses would have spoken would have been just as effective as the *rod* of Moses.

As a result, Moses and Aaron were told that they would be barred from entering into the land. Their lifelong dream died.

Incredible! One sin of anger, one act of disobedience, and the desire of their hearts lay shattered at their feet. For forty years they had talked about Canaan, and now their feet could not enter. They would not be allowed to finish the very task they were called to do. Death—an untimely death—would intervene before they could put a period at the end of the sentence they had been writing.

Was this judgment too severe? From our standpoint, it is hard to believe that God would so discipline Moses for one act of uncontrolled anger. But God never acts without a reason. His discipline exactly fit the offense, even if we don't understand all the details.

For one thing, this rock symbolized Christ. Paul wrote, "For I do not want you to be unaware, brethren, that our fathers were all under the cloud, and all passed through the sea; and all were baptized into Moses in the cloud and in the sea; and all ate the same spiritual food" (1 Cor 10:1-3). Moses was commanded to strike the rock the first time, because Christ was struck on the cross. But after He was put to death, we now must simply speak to the rock to receive its refreshment. He broke this Old Testament type of Christ.

Moses might not have understood this symbolism, but he should have known that it is not necessary for us to know why God gives a command. The Almighty might have hidden reasons that go well beyond the sphere of human understanding. The ultimate intention of His commands are known to Him alone. The Lord said that Moses had not "treated Him as holy."

Second, Moses had such intimacy with God that he knew how important it was for him to obey. He was, after all, the only one to whom God spoke "as a man speaks with his friend." He had been allowed to know God better than any other living man. Disobedience was a violation of that special friendship.

Yes, the water flowed, but this did not mean that God was pleased with what Moses had done. Our pragmatic age must learn that results are not all that matters; for God, the process is often just as important as the end product. *The blessing of God is not always proof of the approval of God.*

Contrary to Scripture, a believer might marry an unbeliever and yet experience the blessing of God. Perhaps the spouse will come to know Christ as Savior and the children will serve God. Yet God is grieved because of the original disobedience.

God in mercy has often appeared to bless disobedience. A pastor who was having an adulterous affair said he was so confused because despite his sin the church continued to grow. Eventually, of course, his sin caught up with him and he paid much more than he could have even dreamed. The lesson to be learned is that we cannot judge an action by its short-term consequences.

Moses was unwilling to take God's no for an answer. As he later explained, he pleaded with God, "'Let me, I pray, cross over and see the fair land that is beyond the Jordan, that good hill country and Lebanon.' But the Lord was angry with me on your account, and would not listen to me; and the Lord said to me, 'Enough! Speak to Me no more of this matter'" (Dt 3:25-26). No matter how much he regretted hitting the rock, he knew that the past could not be changed. He was told to quit praying about it and just accept it. God had spoken so the matter was closed.

Moses Reflects

During those melancholic days, Moses wrote Psalm 90. He reminisces about the meaning of life and how to cope with regrets. He thinks about the faithfulness of God as well as the frailty of man. He meditates on how quickly it has all passed by and how different it could have been.

He begins by contrasting our frailty with God's eternity. "Lord, Thou hast been our dwelling place in all generations. Before the mountains were born, or Thou didst give birth to the earth and the world, even from everlasting to everlasting Thou art God" (Ps 90:1-2). The Almighty existed from all eternity; He was not created, nor did He spontaneously come into existence. He has always been there. And of course, He will exist forever. We can understand eternity future, but we cannot understand eternity past. The idea that God had no beginning is quite unthinkable.

As for man, "Thou dost turn man back into dust. And dost say, 'Return O children of men.' For a thousand years in Thy sight are like yesterday when it passes by, or as a watch in the night" (vv. 3-4). God is always there, but men return to dust. We are like grass that springs up in the morning and fades in the evening. We live a hundred years and think we have lived a good long while, but to God it is like a moment of time. A thousand years is like one day.

Second, he contrasts our sinfulness with God's holiness. Five times he uses the word *anger* or *wrath*. For example, he writes, "For we have been consumed by Thine anger, and by Thy wrath we have been dismayed. Thou hast placed our iniquities before Thee, our secret sins in the light of Thy presence" (vv. 7-8). He is meditating on God's anger with disobedience, perhaps even his own disobedience of smiting the rock. Even our secret sins, he says, are open to the light of God's presence.

No wonder he writes, "So teach us to number our days, that we may present to Thee a heart of wisdom" (v. 12). We should meditate on how few our days are, even as David prayed, "Lord, make me to know my end, and what is the extent of my days, let me know how transient I am" (Ps 39:4). How desperately we need wisdom in knowing how best to use the few days we have.

Moses ends Psalm 90 thinking of our inner longings and our need for God's grace. We yearn for Him but never seem to be satisfied. God has planted eternity in our hearts, yet we look around and see nothing but change and decay. The works of our hands are soon obliterated; we are not long remembered after our death. We are frustrated because, try as we might, we cannot achieve the permanence we so desperately long for. "Make us glad according to the days Thou hast afflicted us, and the years we have seen evil. Let Thy work appear to Thy servants, and Thy majesty to their children" (vv. 15-16).

He concludes by saying that yes, we can have permanence if what we do is done for God. "And let the favor of the Lord our God be upon us; and do confirm for us the work of our hands; yes, confirm the work of our hands" (v. 17). At the end of our days, anything that has truly been done for God will remain.

Please note that God satisfied Moses' desires even after his failure in the wilderness. God does not abandon His people when they take long detours in their journey to the Promised Land. When we fail in our outward goals, God begins His work in the heart.

Today we can be reconciled to God because Jesus Christ united dust and deity; He is our representative, our mediator who rightly relates us to God. And He said that even a cup of cold water given in His name would not go unnoticed.

In 1984 a woman named Niro Asistent became very ill with a disease that subjected her body to high fevers and severe chills, accompanied by bouts of trembling. Intense pain spread throughout neck, arms, and legs. The next year, her lover (who did not tell her that he was bisexual) was diagnosed with AIDS. Niro was then diagnosed as HIV positive and told by a counselor that she had eighteen months to live. "I was numb," she said. "Nothing prepares you for this." A few weeks later, she calculated that she had 492 days to live.

But this death sentence became a wake-up call. She wrote, "When I honestly embraced the fact that my immune system was slowly failing me, and that I would die in eighteen months or less, the illusion of living forever like a veil was suddenly ripped off my face." She now understood that, "Each day that passed would never return, something shifted inside of me.

Suddenly each day was precious to me. It was not an intellectual understanding, it was an actual experience of each moment as sacred.... There was no more time to waste dreaming of what would be, or regretting what didn't happen. I was acutely aware that I had a finite number of days remaining on this Earth (as we all do), and chose to reprioritize my life accordingly" (*The Chicago Tribune*, August 22, 1993). She chose to live fully in the moment; to notice the sounds and sights around her and the feelings within her. Incredibly, as of this writing, she is still alive, beating the odds.

How differently we would live if we remembered that we are terminal, that our days are numbered. If we knew our specific number, we would be motivated to make each day count. Of course, God has our days numbered and each evening one more is stricken from the tally. The fact that we don't know how many days we have should be an even greater motivation for living each one for God. Tomorrow may be our last.

Recently I attended the funeral of a man who had left his wife of twenty years in favor of another woman. After the divorces were finalized, they were married, legitimizing their private liaison. Yet incredibly, after just three months of marriage, he died of a heart attack. I couldn't help but think of how differently he would have lived if he had known that he would die so suddenly at a relatively young age. Perhaps he would have stayed with his first wife, no matter how terrible his marriage, if he had known that his trials would soon be over. We can only speculate regarding how such matters will be handled at the Judgment Seat of Christ.

Moses prepared for his death by depositing the book he had written in the ark of the covenant and by training Joshi to take his place. To the end, he exhorted the people v reminders of God's faithfulness and warnings of His judgment. The Book of Deuteronomy is a beautiful blend of history and practical doctrine.

God tempered His judgment of Moses with mercy. He asked His faithful servant to come with Him to Mount Nebo—the top of Pisgah, which is opposite Jericho—and showed him the land north and south and east and west, all the way to the sea. Moses even saw the desert and the palm trees of Jericho. Then he died and God Himself buried him, not entrusting Moses' resting place to any other being, whether man or angel. He died, "by the word of the Lord" at a site unknown, so that people would be forced to turn their attention toward heaven:

> Now Moses went up from the plains of Moab to Mount Nebo, to the top of Pisgah, which is opposite Jericho. And the Lord showed him all the land, Gilead as far as Dan, and all Naphtali and the land of Ephraim and Manasseh, and all the land of Judah as far as the western sea, and the Negev and the plain in the valley of Jericho, the city of palm trees, as far as Zoar. Then the Lord said to him, "This is the land which I swore to Abraham, Isaac, and Jacob, saying, 'I will give it to your descendants'; I have let you see it with your eyes, but you shall not go over there." So Moses the servant of the Lord died there in the land of Moab, according to the word of the Lord. And He buried him in the valley in the land of Moab, opposite Beth-peor; but no man knows his burial place to this day. Although Moses was one hundred and twenty years old when he died, his eye was not dim, nor his vigor abated.
>
> DEUTERONOMY 34:1-7

For reasons unclear to us, the devil himself vied for the body with Michael, God's archangel (Jude 9).

Moses' transgressions had been forgiven. The rod that had been sanctified by God fell still. The man whose prayers had brought the plagues to Egypt and a wind to part the waters of the Red Sea was now dead.

Today Moses beholds the glory of God even more clearly. The man who desired to be as close to God as possible on earth, now is as close as he will ever be in heaven. His life is a vivid reminder that when we forsake the pleasures of sin for a season we are blessed with the riches of God for eternity.